Stop Overthinking for Leaders

A Leading-Edge Guide to Decisive Leadership, Empowering Teams and Driving Strategic Alignment

Bonnie A Ross

Bonnie A Ross Coaching LLC

Disclaimer:

This book is intended to provide general information and strategies for managing overthinking and is not a substitute for professional mental health advice, diagnosis, or treatment. If overthinking is significantly impacting your quality of life, or if you have concerns about your mental health, please seek the guidance of a qualified healthcare provider. The techniques and insights shared herein are meant to complement, not replace, the specialized training and professional judgment of a mental health professional.

This publication is designed to provide accurate and authoritative information regarding the subject matter covered. It is sold with the understanding that neither the author nor the publisher is engaged in rendering legal, investment, accounting, or other professional services. While the publisher and author have used their best efforts in preparing this book, they make no representations or warranties concerning the accuracy or completeness of the book's contents and specifically disclaim any implied warranties of merchantability or fitness for a particular purpose. Sales representatives or written sales materials may create or extend no warranty. The advice and strategies contained herein may not be suitable for your situation. You should consult with a professional when appropriate. Neither the publisher nor the author shall be liable for any loss of profit or any other commercial damages, including but not limited to special, incidental, consequential, personal, or other damages.

First edition 2024

Contents

Dedication

To My Dear Friend, Edison

To my Huckleberry, my joy and pride,
Through every journey, you're by my side.
Your snuggles soothe, your antics delight,
With you, dear Edison, life is bright.

Photobombing

Epigraph

"Leadership is not about titles, positions, or flowcharts. It is about one life influencing another."

– John C. Maxwell

Introduction

Reflecting on what it means to be a leader in modern times, I realize that despite my extensive leadership experience, I have not fully appreciated the mental and holistic demands required to navigate the path to success. The constant pressure to make impactful decisions, the weight of responsibility, and the fear of failure often lead to a debilitating cycle of overthinking. This realization was the catalyst for writing this book. I wanted to address leaders' unique challenges and provide actionable strategies to overcome overthinking. Let me share with you the insights from this reflection and the inspiration that shaped *Stop Overthinking for Leaders: A Guide to Decisive Leadership, Advancing Team Excellence, and Maximizing Impact.*

In today's rapidly evolving workplace, marked by relentless speed, complexity, and demands for innovation, the challenges leaders face are ever-shifting and increasingly complex. This dynamic environment requires leaders to assess, adjust, and refine their strategies continually. These modern demands are not typically learned through traditional training but are honed through hands-on experience, meaning that learning is often the by-product of unexpected outcomes, unfortunately often labeled "failures."

The mind of a leader is both a sanctuary and a battlefield. Here, decisions are not merely made but forged under immense pressure and responsibility. The essence of leadership lies not only in making decisions but in ensuring these decisions are timely and of high quality. Every leader strives for excellence, yet this pursuit can paradoxically lead to overthinking due to their roles' intricate demands and responsibilities.

At its core, leadership involves making decisions that significantly impact organizations, stakeholders, and individual careers. This weight of responsibility often leads to persistent reevaluation of decisions, scenarios, and outcomes. Leaders might ruminate on potential risks and consequences, striving to foresee and mitigate any negative impacts. The desire to make the perfect choice can stall decision-making processes and lead to overanalysis, especially in complex or high-pressure situations.

Leaders also face the challenge of uncertainty, an inherent aspect of any leadership role. The future can never be predicted accurately, and this uncertainty can be fertile ground for overthinking. Leaders often try to prepare for every possible scenario, leading to exhaustive analyses and contingency planning. While being prepared is a key leadership trait, excessive focus on what might go wrong can distract from immediate and achievable goals, spread resources too thin, and create inefficiency.

The visibility and scrutiny that come with leadership positions also contribute to overthinking. Leaders are often in the spotlight, where their decisions, successes, and failures are observed and critiqued by many. The pressure to maintain a favorable public image and uphold the organization's reputation can lead leaders to overthink communications and strategic moves. The fear of public criticism or stakeholder disapproval can exacerbate this, leading to overly cautious decision-making that prioritizes safety over innovation or necessary risk-taking.

Lastly, the complex interpersonal dynamics of leading diverse teams can lead to overthinking. Leaders must navigate varying personalities, expectations, and communication styles. Balancing assertiveness with empathy, providing clear direction while encouraging autonomy, and resolving conflicts while maintaining team cohesion can be daunting. Leaders may overanalyze conversations, feedback, and team interactions, concerned about maintaining harmony and motivating their teams effectively. While fundamental, this concern can sometimes lead to paralysis by analysis in leadership practices.

If you are currently a leader, you are already successful, and I hope to help you elevate your leadership to the next level. If you are developing skills to become a leader, I celebrate your thoughtful, proactive skill-building. Investing in personal and professional growth as a leader is admirable and has a ripple effect well beyond your own journey.

I am Bonnie A. Ross, and I have navigated the challenges of corporate leadership, delved into the depths of holistic healing, and emerged as a guide for those who seek to lead with their minds and hearts. My journey from an executive at The Walt Disney Company to an identity coach has given me a unique perspective, blending the rigors of corporate leadership with the insights of neuro-linguistic programming (NLP), Reiki Mastery, Quantum Human Design ™, and more. This book is a confluence of my journey, learning, and desire to empower leaders like you.

Stop Overthinking for Leaders is not just a book; it's a guide designed to arm you with actionable strategies to enhance your decision-making, boost your team's confidence, and skyrocket productivity. Backed by scientific research and enriched by personal experience, this book promises a transformative journey from overthinking to decisive action.

In the high demands of leadership, quick, efficient thinking isn't just an asset; it's a necessity. Data and research underscore the perils of overthinking—delayed decisions, missed opportunities, and dwindling team morale. This book addresses these challenges head-on, offering a practical, dual-purpose design that serves as a comprehensive guide and a quick reference to navigate the hurdles of overthinking.

This book is for leaders from all walks of life who seek to sharpen their quick-thinking abilities through strategies that are as scientifically sound as they are applicable. Drawing upon a broad spectrum of disciplines, from neuro-linguistic programming to energy medicine, this guide offers a holistic approach to conquering overthinking, ensuring that you lead with confidence, clarity, and purpose.

Welcome to *Stop Overthinking for Leaders*—your path to decisive leadership and heightened productivity begins now.

I

Why We Overthink

Marcus Aurelius: "You have power over your mind – not outside events. Realize this, and you will find strength."

O verthinking is a prevalent issue among leaders, driven by a deep-seated desire to avoid pain and discomfort while striving for success. This mental habit often leads us away from practical solutions and into a maze of excessive worry and speculation. At the root, overthinking frequently revolves around our attempts to out-think emotions and fears, attempting to solve problems to avoid repeating past mistakes and pains preemptively. While seemingly logical, this approach is fundamentally flawed and can be emotionally exhausting, creating a complex landscape where every decision feels critical, and the margin for error seems nonexistent.

In the context of leadership, overthinking often begins as a protective measure—a way for us to control every variable to ensure imagined catastrophes or past discomforts are not experienced. We may believe that by predicting and preparing for every outcome, we can avoid failure and emotional pain. This leads to a relentless cycle of rumination where the mind continuously tries to solve unsolvable puzzles. The pressure to succeed, care for the company, deliver for clients and stakeholders, and empower and advance our teams exacerbates this tendency.

A significant driver behind overthinking is the quest for perfection. We typically seek the 'perfect' solution that accounts for all possible outcomes, aiming to create a future where discomfort is minimized and risks are mitigated. However, pursuing a perfect solution is futile because life and business are inherently unpredictable. This quest only sets us up for frustration and disappointment when outcomes inevitably deviate from the calculated scenarios.

Another significant cause of overthinking is the belief that we must know everything before taking the first step. This mindset is common yet misguided. In today's rapidly evolving business landscape, the pace of change has increased dramatically, rendering the traditional large-scale planning approach obsolete. Companies embrace agile methodologies prioritizing adaptability, iterative progress, and real-time problem-solving over exhaustive pre-planning. This shift acknowledges that it is impossible to foresee every variable or challenge and emphasizes the importance of flexibility and responsiveness. When we cling to the outdated notion of needing complete knowledge before acting, we often find ourselves paralyzed by indecision, missing opportunities for innovation and growth.

The role of leaders is also evolving from a top-down, command-and-control approach to a highly collaborative one. Modern leadership often involves guiding teams with talents and expertise we do not possess. This shift requires us to rely on and trust our team members, further intensifying the potential for overthinking as we navigate unfamiliar territories and the complexities of shared decision-making.

Overthinking is an incredibly taxing mental process. Constantly analyzing possibilities, imagining outcomes, and strategizing against threats consume significant mental energy. This form of mental exertion doesn't just deplete cognitive resources; it can lead to decision fatigue, stress, and even burnout. Ironically, the more we try to avoid discomfort through overthinking, the more likely we are to create a state of ongoing mental and emotional discomfort.

A critical aspect of overthinking is its anchoring in past experiences. We often use past pain as a benchmark for what must be avoided in the future, keeping us tethered to those very discomforts. By continuously focusing on past negative experiences or imagined catastrophes in the future, we fail to make room for new, potentially positive experiences. We remain stuck in a loop where past fears dictate future choices, limiting professional growth and emotional resilience.

Overthinking differs from normal reflection or future planning in its intensity and negative impact on our well-being. For us, this means it can hinder decision-making, reduce creativity, and impair the ability to lead effectively. Scientific research indicates that overthinking can lead to anxiety and depression, further complicating the already challenging responsibilities of leadership.

Understanding the unique challenges of leadership in the modern world validates the prevalence of overthinking. We must navigate a rapidly changing environment, manage diverse teams, and balance the demands of multiple stakeholders. This intricate web of responsibilities and the high stakes involved make overthinking a common, albeit counterproductive, response. However, while overthinking can be overwhelming, solutions are available to help us navigate these challenges and foster more effective and balanced decision-making.

2

Distinguishing Overthinking from OCD and ADHD

"To know thyself is the beginning of wisdom." –
Socrates

L et's take a moment to learn and empower ourselves with the knowledge to distinguish between overthinking, Obsessive-Compulsive Disorder (OCD), and Attention-Deficit/Hyperactivity Disorder (ADHD). Proper grounding in mental health literacy is essential for effective support and intervention. Understanding these distinctions ensures that we do not trivialize serious conditions or mislabel everyday experiences, which can lead to inadequate care and support. The overuse of some terms stems from the practice using terms like OCD and ADHD to describe behaviors that may resemble these conditions superficially, but without recognizing the clinical criteria and severity involved.

Proper grounding in the nuances of these terms allows us to approach mental health with greater precision, fostering an environment where individuals seek the most appropriate and effective interventions. This knowledge empowers us to advocate for ourselves and others, promoting a culture of awareness and acceptance that is crucial for addressing mental health challenges with the sensitivity and accuracy they require.

Understanding the Difference Between Overthinking and OCD

In everyday conversations, it's not uncommon to hear people casually refer to themselves as being "OCD" when they are simply meticulous or "overthinkers." While these terms are often used interchangeably, this practice can lead to misunderstandings about the nature of overthinking and OCD. Misusing these terms can trivialize the experiences of those who genuinely suffer from OCD and muddle the understanding of what overthinking truly entails. To determine whether someone has OCD or is simply an overthinker, consider the frequency and intensity of the thoughts and behaviors, the impact on daily life, and the level of emotional distress caused. Let's take a closer look to learn more.

Overthinking involves excessive rumination and analysis, often focusing on past events, future possibilities, or hypothetical scenarios. While overthinking can be a response to stress or anxiety, it is not classified as a mental disorder. It often manifests as a habit of getting stuck in a loop of negative thoughts and hinders decision-making and problem-solving.

OCD is a chronic mental health condition characterized by unwanted, intrusive thoughts (obsessions) and repetitive behaviors or mental acts (compulsions) performed to reduce the anxiety caused by these obsessions. OCD is a serious condition that can significantly impact a person's daily life and requires professional diagnosis and treatment. Key characteristics of OCD include persistent, intrusive thoughts that cause significant anxiety or distress, repetitive behaviors performed to neutralize or reduce the distress caused by obsessions, and significant interference with daily functioning, causing marked distress and impacting social, occupational, or other important areas of life. According to the National Institute of Mental Health (NIMH), OCD affects approximately 1.2% of the U.S. adult population annually. This statistic highlights that OCD is a relatively rare but impactful condition.

While challenging, overthinking can often be managed with various self-help strategies and lifestyle changes. Mindfulness and meditation techniques can help individuals stay present and reduce the habit of ruminating on past or future events. On the other hand, OCD requires professional intervention, often involving a combination of therapy and medication. Recognizing the difference between overthinking and OCD is vital for providing appropriate support and treatment. Overthinking, while challenging, is often manageable with self-help strategies and lifestyle changes. OCD, on the other hand, is a serious mental health condition requiring professional intervention. Understanding and respecting these differences fosters empathy and supports those who need it most. By educating ourselves on these distinctions and the available treatments, we can better support ourselves and others, ensuring that those who struggle with OCD receive the understanding and treatment they need while also addressing the habits of overthinking in constructive ways.

Understanding the Difference Between Overthinking and ADHD

Another commonly confused term is "ADHD," often used loosely and interchangeably with "overthinking," leading to misunderstandings about their true meanings and implications. While both overthinking and ADHD can affect cognitive processes and behavior, they are distinct conditions with unique characteristics and treatments. This section aims to clarify the differences, explore the prevalence of ADHD, and provide insights into recognizing and respecting these differences.

As previously discussed, overthinking involves excessive rumination and analysis, often focusing on past events, future possibilities, or hypothetical scenarios. On the other hand, ADHD is a neurodevelopmental disorder characterized by persistent patterns of inattention, hyperactivity, and impulsivity that interfere with daily functioning. ADHD is commonly diagnosed in childhood but can continue into adulthood. It is a condition that requires professional diagnosis and management. Key characteristics of ADHD include difficulty sustaining attention, frequent fidgeting or restlessness, impulsive behavior, and challenges with organizing tasks and activities. According to the Centers for Disease Control and Prevention (CDC), ADHD affects approximately 4.4% of U.S. adults.

While both overthinking and ADHD can lead to difficulties in focusing and completing tasks, their underlying mechanisms and manifestations are different. Overthinking is often driven by anxiety and a desire to control outcomes through excessive thought. It involves voluntary, though excessive, contemplation and worry about various aspects of life. Overthinkers tend to be mentally exhausted from continuous thought processes but generally have the capacity to focus when necessary.

In contrast, ADHD is characterized by involuntary patterns of inattention, hyperactivity, and impulsivity that make it difficult to focus or complete tasks. People with ADHD often struggle with executive functions, such as organizing, planning, and sustaining attention on tasks that require prolonged mental effort. Unlike overthinking, ADHD is not a voluntary pattern and significantly impairs daily functioning across various settings, such as at work, school, or home.

Misunderstanding the differences between overthinking and ADHD can result in inappropriate self-diagnosis or treatment. While overthinking, though challenging, can often be managed with self-help strategies and lifestyle adjustments, ADHD is a serious neurodevelopmental disorder that requires professional intervention. By educating ourselves on these distinctions and the available treatments, we can better assist ourselves and others, ensuring that individuals with ADHD receive the necessary understanding and treatment while also constructively addressing overthinking habits.

3
Common Overthinking Challenges

"You are braver than you believe, stronger than you seem, and smarter than you think." – A.A. Milne

Most overthinkers share five common challenges: analysis paralysis, fear of failure, decision fatigue, cognitive bias, and unmanaged stress. While these challenges manifest uniquely within each overthinker, their core impacts remain consistent. Understanding these shared struggles is crucial for developing effective strategies to manage overthinking and enhance leadership efficacy.

Analysis Paralysis

Analysis paralysis is a state of overthinking and excessive analysis that prevents decision-making or taking action. It occurs when the focus on considering all possible outcomes, variables, and data points becomes so overwhelming that forward movement becomes impossible.

The impact of analysis paralysis can have significant negative consequences for individuals and organizations. For leaders, it can result in missed opportunities, stalled projects, and an inability to respond effectively to changes and challenges. Teams may become frustrated by the lack of direction and momentum, leading to decreased morale and productivity. On a personal level, analysis paralysis can cause stress, anxiety, and a sense of being overwhelmed.

The desire for absolute certainty before making a decision often drives analysis paralysis. Many believe that a perfect outcome can be ensured if enough information is gathered and all possible scenarios are considered. However, this desire for certainty is unrealistic and impossible to achieve, leading to endless thinking and no action. The fear of making a mistake or facing negative consequences can be paralyzing. Worrying about the repercussions of a wrong decision, such as failure, criticism, or lost opportunities, can drive the need to seek more information and consider more options, deepening the paralysis.

In today's world, it's easy to be flooded with data. Filtering and prioritizing this information can be challenging, leading to cognitive overload. The sheer volume of data can make it hard to see the bigger picture and make timely decisions. A lack of self-confidence can also exacerbate overthinking. Those who doubt their decision-making abilities may constantly seek external validation and second-guess their choices. This lack of confidence prevents trust in one's judgment and ability to take decisive action.

Strategies to Overcome Analysis Paralysis

- **Set Clear Deadlines:** Establish firm deadlines for decisions to prevent endless analysis. Set a reasonable timeframe for gathering information and commit to making a decision by that date.

- **Limit Information Intake:** Identify the most critical pieces of information needed to make an informed decision and focus on those. Avoid the temptation to gather every possible data point.

- **Prioritize Decisions:** Not all decisions are equally important. Prioritize decisions based on their impact and urgency, and allocate time and energy accordingly.

- **Embrace Imperfection:** Accept that no decision is perfect and that mistakes are part of the learning process. Focus on making the best decision with available information, and be prepared to adjust if needed.

- **Build Confidence:** Trust your judgment and decision-making abilities. Seek feedback and validation when necessary, but learn to rely on instincts and experience.

- **Practice Decisiveness:** Create a habit of making small decisions quickly and confidently. This practice can help build the decision-making muscle and reduce the tendency to overthink.

Overcoming analysis paralysis requires a deliberate shift in mindset, embracing action over perfection, and fostering a supportive environment for decision-making. By recognizing and addressing the underlying causes of overthinking, leaders can cultivate a more agile and resilient approach to challenges. Remember, progress is achieved one step at a time, and each decision, no matter how small, propels you forward on your leadership journey.

Fear of Failure

The fear of failure is an intense apprehension about the possibility of negative outcomes, mistakes, or unfavorable judgments that can paralyze action or decision-making. This fear often stems from the perceived consequences of failure, ranging from personal embarrassment to professional setbacks.

For leaders, this fear can result in a reluctance to take necessary risks, a lack of innovation, and a tendency to avoid decisive moves. This can lead to a culture of caution and risk aversion within teams, stifling creativity and growth. On a personal level, the fear of failure can cause chronic stress, anxiety, and a diminished sense of self-worth.

The fear of failure arises from several factors. High expectations, whether self-imposed or external, can make failing seem unacceptable. Unrealistically high goals can create immense pressure to achieve perfection. Past experiences, such as negative events or harsh criticism, can leave a lasting impact, making the prospect of repeating mistakes daunting.

Perceived consequences play a significant role. Fear of potential negative outcomes, like losing respect, damaging one's reputation, or facing actual losses, can be overwhelming. These potential consequences are often exaggerated, making failure appear catastrophic.

Self-doubt exacerbates the fear of failure. Lack of confidence in one's abilities increases the likelihood of being paralyzed by the thought of making mistakes. This lack of confidence can prevent taking action, further intensifying the fear.

Strategies to Overcome Fear of Failure

- **Shift Perspective:** Reframe failure as a learning opportunity rather than a catastrophe. Embrace mistakes as part of the growth process and focus on lessons learned from each experience.

- **Set Realistic Goals:** Establish achievable and realistic goals that allow for incremental progress. Celebrate small successes to build confidence and reduce the pressure of perfection.

- **Cultivate Self-Compassion:** Practice self-compassion and kindness. Recognize that everyone makes mistakes and that imperfection is part of the human experience.

- **Visualize Success:** Instead of focusing on potential failure, visualize successful outcomes. Use positive imagery and affirmations to build confidence and reduce anxiety. Ask yourself, "What could go right?" when overwhelmed by thoughts of failure.

- **Embrace Agility:** Understand that decisions are rarely final or fatal. Develop skills of assessment and refinement to move quickly to the next proactive step when faced with challenges.

- **Take Incremental Risks:** Start by taking small, manageable risks to build resilience and confidence. Gradually increase the level of risk as comfort with potential failure grows.

- **Seek Support:** Surround yourself with a supportive network encouraging risk-taking and providing constructive feedback. Mentorship and peer support can help mitigate the fear of failure.

Overcoming the fear of failure requires a shift in perspective, viewing setbacks as opportunities for growth rather than definitive defeats. Embracing a mindset of continuous learning and resilience enables leaders to navigate challenges with confidence and adaptability. By fostering a culture that values effort and innovation, leaders can diminish the paralyzing grip of fear, paving the way for sustained success and personal fulfillment.

Decision Fatigue

Decision fatigue is the mental exhaustion and diminished capacity to make decisions after a prolonged decision-making period. As cognitive resources are depleted throughout the day, the quality of decisions tends to deteriorate, leading to suboptimal choices or decision avoidance.

Decision fatigue can have significant consequences for both individuals and organizations. For leaders, it results in impaired judgment, an increased likelihood of defaulting to the easiest option, and a tendency to postpone important decisions. This can lead to poor strategic choices, reduced productivity, and weakened team morale. On a personal level, decision fatigue can cause stress, frustration, and a sense of being overwhelmed.

Several factors contribute to decision fatigue. Constant decision-making, from minor to significant choices, depletes mental energy. Complex and important decisions require more mental effort, leading to exhaustion. Lack of prioritization makes every choice seem equally important, creating a sense of overwhelm. Overcommitment spreads cognitive resources too thin, and high expectations add pressure to make perfect decisions, further exhausting mental capacity.

Strategies to Overcome Decision Fatigue

- **Prioritize Decisions:** Identify and focus on the most important decisions first. By prioritizing high-impact decisions, you can allocate cognitive resources more effectively and reduce mental fatigue.

- **Set Decision-Making Boundaries:** Establish specific times of the day for making decisions, preferably when most alert and mentally fresh. Avoid making significant decisions when tired or stressed.

- **Delegate Decisions:** Delegate routine and less critical decisions to others to lighten the cognitive load. Empowering team members to make decisions can also improve their engagement and development.

- **Simplify Choices:** Set criteria for decision-making to reduce the number of options to consider. Simplifying choices conserves mental energy and streamlines the decision-making process.

- **Take Breaks:** Schedule regular breaks throughout the day to recharge mental energy. Short breaks can help prevent cognitive overload and improve overall decision quality.

- **Develop Routines:** Establish routines for recurring decisions to minimize cognitive effort. For example, making budget decisions on Thursday mornings means not having to think about budget related decisions the rest of the week. Having routine decisions be routine can free up mental resources for more complex decisions.

Overcoming decision fatigue requires a strategic approach prioritizing self-awareness, mindful practices, and delegation. Leaders can enhance their decision-making capabilities and effectiveness by recognizing the signs of decision fatigue and implementing practical solutions. Fostering a balanced and resilient mindset will empower leaders to navigate their responsibilities more clearly and confidently.

Cognitive Bias

Cognitive bias occurs when judgments systematically deviate from rationality, leading to illogical conclusions or decisions. These biases, acting as mental shortcuts, simplify complex decision-making processes but often result in errors. They can significantly skew perception and decision-making, leading to flawed strategies, missed opportunities, and poor team dynamics.

As leaders, cognitive biases may result in a lack of objectivity, reinforcing preexisting fears and anxieties and creating a feedback loop that perpetuates overthinking. Additionally, cognitive biases can undermine team trust and collaboration if decisions appear inconsistent or unfair.

These biases occur because the brain seeks to simplify information processing in a complex world. They help make quick decisions but at the cost of accuracy. For overthinkers, who are already prone to excessive analysis and anxiety, relying on these mental shortcuts more heavily can reinforce preexisting fears and anxieties.

Types of Cognitive Bias in Overthinking

Several cognitive biases commonly affect overthinkers, including:

- **Confirmation Bias**: The tendency to search for, interpret, and remember information in a way that confirms preexisting beliefs. Overthinkers may selectively gather information supporting their fears and anxieties while ignoring data contradicting them.

- **Negativity Bias**: The tendency to focus more on negative experiences and information than positive ones. This bias can exacerbate anxiety and pessimism, leading to a skewed perception of reality.

- **Status Quo Bias**: The preference for the current state of affairs and resistance to change. Overthinkers may avoid making decisions that could disrupt the status quo, even if change is necessary.

- **Anchoring Bias**: The tendency to rely too heavily on the first piece of information encountered (the "anchor") when making decisions. Overthinkers may fixate on initial data points and find it difficult to adjust their thinking as new information becomes available.

"WADIT WAY" Bias

Ok, I made this one up, but just like Nessie and the Yeti, you become a believer when you see it. The phrase "We've always done it this way" (WADIT Way) signals the presence of a particular status quo cognitive bias common to established organizations. This mindset can stifle innovation, limit growth, and prevent adaptation to changing environments because it is hard to argue that something was effective in the past. Additionally, it fosters a culture of comfort and familiarity that overshadows the need for improvement and adaptation. Leaders who allow this bias to persist may find their teams resistant to change, ultimately hindering the organization's ability to evolve and stay competitive. The challenge lies in recognizing that what worked in the past may not be suitable for future challenges and opportunities.

Mitigating cognitive biases is crucial for making quality decisions, especially in leadership roles where the impact of choices extends beyond individual outcomes to influence entire teams and organizations. By recognizing and addressing cognitive biases, leaders can enhance their decision-making processes, ensuring they are grounded in rationality and objectivity rather than flawed shortcuts. This proactive approach helps to prevent errors that arise from irrational judgments.

Strategies to Overcoming Cognitive Bias

- **Seek Diverse Perspectives**: Encourage input from various sources to counteract personal biases. Diverse perspectives can provide a more balanced view and challenge existing assumptions.

- **Use Structured Decision-Making Processes**: Implement structured decision-making frameworks that require consideration of multiple viewpoints and data sources. This can help mitigate the influence of cognitive biases.

- **Practice Mindfulness**: Develop mindfulness practices to become more aware of personal biases and their impact on decision-making. Mindfulness can help create a mental space to evaluate information more objectively.

- **Challenge Assumptions**: Regularly question and challenge assumptions. Ask what evidence supports your beliefs and consider alternative viewpoints.

- **Educate Yourself on Cognitive Biases**: Learn about common cognitive biases and their effects. Awareness is the first step towards mitigating their impact.

- **Encourage Open Dialogue**: Foster a culture of open dialogue and constructive feedback within the team. Encourage team members to speak up if they notice biases influencing decisions.

Navigating this bias requires leaders to foster a culture of critical thinking and openness to change. Encouraging team members to question existing processes and explore new ideas can break the inertia of the status quo. This involves creating an environment where experimentation is valued, and failure is seen as a learning opportunity rather than a setback. Leaders must model this behavior themselves, demonstrating a willingness to embrace change and take calculated risks. By actively seeking diverse perspectives and promoting a culture of continuous improvement, leaders can mitigate the effects of status quo bias and drive their organizations forward.

Additionally, leveraging data and evidence to challenge the "we've always done it this way" mentality is crucial. Presenting clear, data-driven insights highlighting new approaches' potential benefits can make a compelling case for change. Engaging the team in the decision-making process and providing opportunities for them to contribute ideas can also build buy-in and reduce resistance. Through transparent communication and a focus on the tangible benefits of innovation, leaders can guide their teams through the discomfort of change, ensuring the organization remains dynamic and resilient in the face of evolving challenges.

Unmanaged Stress

Unmanaged stress accumulates physical, emotional, and mental strain without effective coping mechanisms, leading to a state of chronic stress. When stressors are not addressed and managed, overwhelming pressure ensues.

This chronic condition has significant negative consequences on both personal and professional levels. It can impair decision-making, reduce resilience, and negatively affect team morale. Health issues such as anxiety, depression, cardiovascular problems, and a weakened immune system are common due to chronic stress. In the workplace, unmanaged stress can decrease productivity, increase absenteeism, and result in higher turnover rates.

Several reasons contribute to unmanaged stress. High expectations often cause stress. Setting very high standards for oneself and others leads to constant pressure to be perfect and avoid mistakes. Another issue is a lack of boundaries. Difficulty saying no and taking on too many tasks leaves little time for rest.

Additionally, poor time management can exacerbate stress. Spending too much time planning and thinking, with insufficient time for doing things and self-care, is detrimental. Emotional suppression is another contributing factor. Hiding feelings and avoiding dealing with problems directly cause stress to build up and affect health.

Lastly, the fear of appearing weak can prevent effective stress management. Worrying that asking for help makes one look weak or inadequate leads to avoiding steps to handle stress. These combined factors contribute to the overwhelming stress that over-thinkers often experience.

Strategies to Heal Unmanaged Stress

- **Set Realistic Goals:** Establish achievable goals and expectations. Break larger tasks into smaller, manageable steps to reduce feeling overwhelmed.

- **Create Boundaries:** Learn to set and maintain boundaries. Allocate specific times for work, rest, and personal activities to ensure a balanced lifestyle.

- **Practice Time Management:** Develop effective time management skills. Prioritize tasks, delegate when possible, and use tools like calendars and to-do lists to stay organized.

- **Address Emotions:** Acknowledge and address emotions rather than suppressing them. Consider practices such as journaling, meditation, or talking to a trusted friend or therapist.

- **Seek Support:** Don't hesitate to seek support from colleagues, mentors, or mental health professionals. Recognizing that everyone experiences stress and seeking help is a sign of strength, not weakness.

- **Engage in Self-Care:** Incorporate regular self-care activities into your routine. Exercise, hobbies, and relaxation techniques can help manage stress levels and improve overall well-being.

Overcoming unmanaged stress starts with self-awareness and the willingness to make consistent, positive changes. By implementing practical strategies, such as mindfulness, physical activity, and prioritizing self-care, leaders can transform their stress into a manageable and even beneficial force. One can ultimately pave the way for a more balanced, resilient, and fulfilling leadership experience by embracing these practices.

4

Understanding Your Overthinking Type

"Until you make the unconscious conscious, it will direct your life and you will call it fate." – Carl Jung

U nderstanding your overthinking type gives us insight into how you typically respond to the pressures and demands of decision-making. This overthinking type isn't an inherent trait of who you are; rather, it is a pattern of behavior that often manifests as a stress response when faced with important choices and leadership challenges. Over time, you might develop a specific style of overthinking due to past experiences, environmental pressures, or personal insecurities about performance and outcomes.

Recognizing your pattern of overthinking is pivotal in developing strategies to mitigate it. This section aims to illuminate the various types of overthinking leaders might encounter and offers a self-assessment tool designed to pinpoint your unique overthinking tendencies. Armed with this insight, we can tailor strategies that directly address specific challenges, enhancing your decision-making process and leadership effectiveness.

Overthinking Type Assessment

Please note: The References section contains a QR code and URL for downloading personal copies of all assessments and work-sheets. After reading each statement, rate how often you feel or act in the described manner:

Points:

0 – Never

1 – Rarely

2 – Sometimes

3 – Often

4 – Always

Assessment Statements

1. I spend a lot of time ensuring that every detail of my decision is correct before I commit to it.

2. I repeatedly review data and feedback to find the best possible course of action.

3. I often think about all the things that could go wrong with a decision more than its potential benefits.

4. The thought of something going wrong because of a decision I make keeps me up at night.

5. I struggle to make decisions quickly and often feel I need more time to consider all possible options.

6. Even after deciding, I often revisit and doubt it, wondering if I considered everything.

7. I delay making decisions, hoping that more information will become available or the situation will change.

8. I prefer to wait until the last minute to make decisions, which gives me more time to think things over.

9. I aim for perfection in the outcomes of my decisions and worry about falling short of my own or others' expectations.

10. I tend to focus on potential failures more than the possibilities of success.

11. I frequently ask for opinions from others to help make up my mind.

12. I often find excuses for not deciding, even when sufficient information is available.

Scoring

___**The Perfectionist:** Add the scores of statements 1, 2, 9.

___**The Catastrophizer:** Add the scores of statements 3, 4, 10.

___**The Indecisive:** Add the scores of statements 5, 6, 11.

___**The Procrastinator:** Add the scores of statements 7, 8, 12.

Results

High Tendency: If your score in any category is 10 or higher, you likely exhibit many of the characteristics of this leadership style in decision-making.

Moderate Tendency: Scores between 7 and 9 suggest you sometimes display these tendencies.

Low Tendency: Scores of 6 and below indicate occasional behavior aligned with this leadership style.

Refer to the Scoring section if you have two types that scored equally as your dominant overthinking type. The types are listed in a specific order. For example, if you score equally as a Perfectionist and a Procrastinator, your dominant type is Perfectionist because it appears first in the list.

Now that you have completed the assessment and identified your dominant overthinking type, it's time to explore it further.

Insight to Hybrid Types

Overthinking doesn't manifest in a universal form; it adapts to the contours of individual minds, influenced by experiences, responsibilities, and fears. Therefore, it is common to exhibit a hybrid style, combining traits from more than one overthinking type. This blending occurs as diverse situations draw out different aspects of decision making tendencies. Understanding these types is crucial because it helps recognize the behaviors that could negatively influence leadership effectiveness, particularly under stress.

While focusing on the dominant type, it is worth appreciating that there are likely influences from secondary overthinking types. Hybrids typically form as adaptations to environments, challenges, and the repercussions of decisions. Blending different overthinking styles can be a defensive adaptation to past failures, criticisms, or pressures of high-stakes leadership roles. Hybrid styles might also develop due to inherent personality traits being magnified by professional roles. For example, a naturally cautious person in a high-risk industry might become a Perfectionist and a Catastrophizer.

Additionally, leadership demands often require balancing multiple perspectives and competing priorities, which can naturally lead to the development of hybrid styles. For instance, the need to foresee potential problems (Catastrophizer) while struggling with indecision (Indecisive) can merge into a complex leadership approach. Over time, these hybrids can become deeply ingrained if they are perceived to effectively manage specific challenges, despite their potential drawbacks regarding team dynamics, decision-making efficiency, and personal well-being.

Developing a hybrid of more than one overthinking type is not uncommon, as behaviors are influenced by various experiences, personality traits, and environmental pressures. These hybrids can emerge due to overlapping traits from different types, the complexity of roles, or the diverse challenges faced in leadership journeys.

Common Hybrid Types:

The Perfectionist-Procrastinator: This hybrid occurs when the drive for flawless outcomes leads to delays in decisions, waiting for the perfect moment or the most complete set of information. Leaders in this category are meticulous and hesitant to commit until they feel certain about the perfection of their choices. This can result from environments where the consequences of errors are highly punitive, which emphasizes thoroughness while simultaneously fostering a fear of potential mistakes, leading to delays.

The Catastrophizer-Indecisive: Those embodying both the Catastrophizer and Indecisive styles tend to see potential pitfalls in every decision and feel overwhelmed, making it difficult to commit to any action. This hybrid often develops in highly volatile environments where past decisions have unpredictable outcomes, increasing focus on negative possibilities and anxiety about making the wrong choice.

The Perfectionist-Catastrophizer: A combination of striving for flawless decisions while focusing heavily on avoiding negative outcomes, these individuals are extremely cautious. They seek to eliminate errors and are preoccupied with considering everything that could go wrong. This hybrid may form in high-stakes industries such as finance or healthcare, where precision and risk management are critical, and the cost of failure is substantial.

The Indecisive-Procrastinator: This hybrid style exhibits reluctance to make decisions and a tendency to delay them as much as possible. This can result from a lack of confidence in decision-making abilities or from previous experiences where decisions led to significant negative consequences, fostering a habit of avoiding decision-making altogether.

Healing the dominant overthinking tendency will naturally lead to a reduction in the influences of secondary types. As self-awareness is cultivated and hybrid traits are understood, one becomes better equipped with the knowledge needed to show kindness to those aspects of the mind that need it most. This journey is not just about overcoming overthinking; it's about tapping into higher confidence and authenticity. Embrace this process with compassion and patience, and watch as self-knowledge empowers a more balanced and fulfilling life.

Next Steps in Overcoming Overthinking

The previous chapter covered the high-level challenges common to all overthinkers. Now, it's time to identify the unique characteristics of each type of overthinker. Each type has distinct triggers, challenges, strategies for managing overthinking, and a lived experience from a real person who has navigated similar challenges. These insights and stories may resonate with your journey and provide practical guidance on your path to overcoming overthinking.

- **The Perfectionist:** *Turn to Chapter 5.* This chapter explores the Perfectionist's quest for flawlessness, common triggers, and strategies to embrace imperfection. You'll also read about a real-life Perfectionist's experience and how they learned to let go of their need for perfection.

- **The Indecisive:** *Turn to Chapter 6.* This chapter delves into the Indecisive individual's struggle with making decisions, the underlying causes of their hesitation, and effective techniques to build decision-making confidence. A real person's story will illustrate how they overcame indecision and found clarity.

- **The Catastrophizer:** *Turn to Chapter 7.* This chapter addresses the Catastrophizer's tendency to anticipate the worst-case scenarios, the factors fueling these thoughts, and methods to shift towards a more balanced perspective. A lived experience shared in this chapter will highlight the journey from catastrophizing to calmness.

- **The Procrastinator:** *Turn to Chapter 8.* This chapter examines the Procrastinator's habit of delaying tasks, its psychological reasons, and actionable steps to boost productivity. A real Procrastinator's story will provide insights into overcoming procrastination and achieving goals.

Each chapter is designed to provide a comprehensive understanding of your dominant overthinking type, practical strategies to heal it, and relatable experiences that offer hope and inspiration. Embrace this journey with curiosity and without judgment, knowing that each step you take brings you closer to a more balanced and fulfilling life.

5

The Perfectionist Overthinker

My New Mantra: I Embrace Excellence Over Perfection

P erfectionists have a remarkable commitment to excellence, often driving them to pay meticulous attention to detail. This dedication ensures that every task they tackle meets the highest standards, leading to exceptional work that inspires those around them. At the same time, this intense focus on perfection can sometimes spiral into overthinking, creating unnecessary stress and delays.

Imagine being constantly critical of your own work, always feeling the need to tweak and refine every detail. This desire for perfection can be exhausting, as you might find yourself stuck in an endless loop of adjustments, never feeling satisfied. The pressure to meet high expectations from yourself or others can weigh heavily, leading to stress and fatigue. Does this resonate with you? If so, you are not alone!

As a perfectionist leader, you might have developed this trait because of past experiences with high stakes and expected flawless outcomes. Perhaps personal insecurities or a professional environment that punished mistakes made you fear errors. You might be someone who sets exceptionally high standards and pays close attention to detail, often pushing yourself and others to strive for the best.

This drive for perfection can have mixed effects on those around you. On one hand, your thoroughness and commitment to quality can lead to outstanding results. On the other hand, the same traits can cause delays and missed opportunities, as decisions take longer to make. Your high standards might also create a pressurized environment, leading to decreased morale and potential burnout among team members who struggle to keep up.

You might find yourself caught in analysis paralysis, endlessly refining plans in search of the perfect solution, which can frustrate those ready to move forward. Fear of failure can be a constant companion, making you overwork and avoid risks that could lead to imperfection. This fear might also make you reluctant to delegate tasks, worrying that others won't meet your exacting standards, which can lead to burnout and missed opportunities for your team's growth.

Decision fatigue is another challenge you face. The relentless pursuit of flawless decisions can exhaust your cognitive resources, making you feel mentally drained and unsure when it's time to make a final choice. For instance, you might spend excessive time selecting the perfect candidate for a job, meticulously analyzing resumes, and conducting multiple rounds of interviews, only to feel overwhelmed when it's time to decide.

Cognitive biases might also contribute to overthinking. You might seek information that supports your high standards while ignoring more practical approaches. Anchoring bias might make you fixate on initial, unrealistic goals, insisting on an overly ambitious project scope despite evidence suggesting a simpler approach would be more effective.

Unmanaged stress is a common problem for you as a perfectionist. The drive to meet unattainably high standards can lead you to overcommit and take on too much work, striving to ensure everything meets your criteria. This relentless pursuit can result in chronic stress, burnout, and health issues, as you might work long hours, constantly refining projects and striving for flawless execution, ultimately taking a toll on your well-being.

Despite these challenges, your drive for excellence is admirable. It consistently pushes you to achieve the highest standards in every endeavor, often leading to remarkable achievements. The key is to embrace the beauty of imperfection and recognize that mistakes are valuable learning opportunities. By shifting your focus from absolute perfection to continuous improvement, you can find balance and reduce the stress of overthinking. Here are some actions that can help you manage your perfectionist tendencies and embrace a healthier, more sustainable approach to excellence:

1. **Set Realistic Goals:** Aim for achievable targets that balance high standards with practicality. Understand that not every task requires perfection; sometimes, good enough is enough.

2. **Prioritize Tasks:** Identify and focus your energy on the most critical tasks. Let go of the need to perfect every minor detail in less important areas.

3. **Embrace Mistakes as Learning Opportunities:** Shift your perspective to see mistakes as valuable lessons rather

than failures. Each mistake is a chance to grow and improve.

4. **Delegate Effectively:** Trust your team and delegate tasks, understanding that different approaches can yield excellent results. This not only reduces your workload but also empowers your team.

5. **Limit Time Spent on Decision-Making:** Set time limits for making decisions to avoid getting stuck in analysis paralysis. Sometimes, a timely decision is better than a perfect one.

6. **Focus on Progress, Not Perfection:** Celebrate small wins and progress rather than fixating on what's imperfect. This positive reinforcement can boost morale and motivation.

7. **Practice Self-Compassion:** Be kind to yourself. Acknowledge your efforts and recognize that perfection is an unrealistic standard. Treat yourself with the same compassion you would offer a friend.

8. **Seek Feedback from Others:** Open yourself to feedback from others. It can provide new perspectives and help you see where you might be overthinking. Constructive criticism is a valuable tool for growth.

9. **Take Breaks to Prevent Burnout:** Regular breaks and downtime are crucial for maintaining mental and physical health. Step away from work to recharge and come back with a fresh perspective.

10. **Celebrate Achievements, No Matter How Small:** Take the time to acknowledge and celebrate your accomplishments. Recognizing your achievements, big or small, can boost your confidence and reduce the constant pressure for perfection.

By implementing these actions, you can harness your drive for excellence while embracing imperfection. This balance can lead to more sustainable success and a healthier, happier you.

As we wrap up this deep dive into self-awareness and growth, let's end with an empowering mantra: "I Embrace Excellence Over Perfection." This simple yet profound statement can transform your mindset and approach to personal and professional challenges. The beauty of this mantra lies in its ability to shift your focus from the unrealistic pursuit of flawlessness to the attainable goal of doing your best. By embracing excellence, you acknowledge your efforts and progress, celebrating the journey rather than fixating on an unattainable ideal.

To get the most from this mantra, repeat it daily, especially during moments of self-doubt or when you feel the pressure to be perfect. Let it remind you that excellence is within your reach and that striving for it allows growth, learning, and the joy of achievement. This shift in perspective will alleviate the burden of perfectionism and cultivate a more compassionate and productive relationship with yourself and your goals.

Understanding and addressing the challenges we face as Perfectionist leaders can change our decisions. Embracing imperfection, managing decision fatigue, overcoming the fear of failure, and easing cognitive overload can help us lead our teams to success without being paralyzed by overthinking.

Lived Experiences: Transforming Perfectionism into Effective Leadership

"Embrace imperfection as a step towards growth; it's in the flaws and missteps that we find our greatest opportunities to learn and excel." – Sarah

Meet Sarah, a marketing director at a tech firm. Sarah is a talented marketing director known for her high standards and attention to detail. However, her Perfectionist tendencies often led to significant delays in decision-making. She spent countless hours analyzing every detail, fearing any mistake could harm her career and the company's reputation. This caused frustration among her team and resulted in missed opportunities.

The struggle reached a peak when a crucial product launch was delayed multiple times. Sarah's relentless pursuit of perfection caused her to second-guess every decision, from the marketing message to the design elements. Her team was growing increasingly frustrated, feeling their hard work was being undermined by endless revisions and tweaks. The company was losing market share to competitors who were faster to market, and the pressure on Sarah was mounting.

Realizing her overthinking was holding the team back, Sarah decided to attend a leadership workshop. She learned about the negative effects of perfectionism and the importance of embracing imperfection. Initially skeptical, Sarah struggled to accept that "good enough" could be an option. However, the mounting evidence of lost opportunities and declining team morale pushed her to make a change.

Sarah started by setting strict time limits for decisions, allowing herself a set amount of time to decide and then moving forward. This was incredibly challenging at first; she constantly felt the urge to extend deadlines to ensure everything was perfect. But with persistence, she began to see the benefits of quicker decision-making.

She also adopted the 80/20 rule, focusing on the most impactful tasks to boost productivity. This shift was difficult, as it meant letting go of some control and trusting that the remaining 20% wouldn't jeopardize the project's success. She began delegating tasks to her team, providing clear guidelines and support. Initially, Sarah found it hard to trust others with critical tasks, fearing they wouldn't meet her standards. But over time, she saw her team rise to the occasion, handling responsibilities competently and even bringing fresh ideas to the table.

Sarah practiced cognitive reframing to address her fear of mistakes, viewing errors as learning opportunities. Encouraging a culture of feedback and continuous improvement within her team helped to reduce the stigma around failure. This cultural shift was slow and met with resistance, but Sarah's commitment gradually fostered a more open and supportive environment.

These changes had a significant impact—projects were completed more efficiently, and team morale improved. The breakthrough came with the timely launch of a marketing campaign that had previously been delayed. By setting clear deadlines, prioritizing key elements, and trusting her team, the campaign launched on time and exceeded expectations, attracting new customers. This success reinvigorated the team and boosted Sarah's confidence in her new approach.

Sarah's story shows how Perfectionist leaders can transform their approach and effectively lead. By setting time limits, prioritizing tasks, delegating, and embracing imperfection, Sarah improved her decision-making and created a more productive and positive work environment. Her journey demonstrates that with the right strategies and perseverance, Perfectionist leaders can overcome overthinking and achieve success, turning their struggles into strengths.

———◦———

Introduction to Reflection Exercise

Journal your responses to the reflection prompts.

Take your time with this exercise. Remember, there is no wrong way to do this. Approach these questions with curiosity and without judgment. Treat it like you are interviewing a close friend. This is an opportunity to gain insight and understanding about your habits and how they impact you and your team.

- **Self-Reflection**: What fears or insecurities drive your need for perfection in your work and decision-making?

- **Identify Strengths and Skills:** What strengths and skills have you cultivated that can help you balance your tendency towards perfectionism? How can you leverage these abilities to take more decisive actions and improve your productivity and leadership?

- **Impact on Team**: How do your high standards and meticulousness affect your team's morale and productivity?

- **Success Memory**: Recall a time when you achieved a successful outcome without overthinking every detail. What did that experience teach you about trust and delegation?

Self-awareness and insights from reflection are transformative tools for personal and professional growth. Like in any relationship, the more intimately we know ourselves, the closer we become to our authentic selves. This deepened understanding fosters greater confidence, clarity, and purpose. Regularly reflecting on our thoughts, behaviors, and patterns reveals profound truths about who we are and what drives us. This journey towards self-discovery enhances our leadership abilities and aligns our actions with our core values, creating a life of genuine fulfillment and integrity.

6

The Indecisive Overthinker

My New Mantra: I Cultivate Confident Decisions

Indecisive overthinkers possess a notable ability to see multiple perspectives and consider various outcomes before making decisions. This thoughtful approach ensures that they weigh all options carefully, often leading to well-rounded and considerate choices that benefit their team and projects. At the same time, this extensive deliberation can sometimes lead to paralysis by analysis, where the fear of making the wrong decision causes unnecessary delays and stress.

Imagine being someone who meticulously considers every option, fearing that the wrong choice could lead to failure or regret. This can be exhausting, as you might spend hours or even days mulling over decisions, big or small. The pressure to make the perfect choice can be paralyzing, leading to stress and second-guessing. Does this resonate with you? If so, you are not alone!

You might have developed this trait as an indecisive leader because of past experiences where decisions led to significant consequences. Perhaps you've faced criticism for your choices or work in an environment that emphasizes flawless decision-making. This fear of making the wrong move can cause you to delay decisions, seek more information or input, and often doubt your own judgment.

This indecisiveness can impact your team in several ways. While it can foster thorough consideration of all options, it can lead to missed opportunities and slow progress. Team members might feel frustrated waiting for decisions, affecting morale and productivity. Your team might also struggle with uncertainty, not knowing what direction to take, creating a tense and unproductive work environment.

Recognizing the dynamics of being an indecisive overthinker starts with understanding your struggle with decision paralysis. You might find yourself caught up in the details, endlessly weighing pros and cons, seeking the perfect solution that may not exist. This can delay progress and frustrate those ready to move forward. For example, you might spend days comparing different software options for a project, unable to commit to one, which delays the entire team's progress.

If you are concerned about failure, you might have a deep-seated dread of making the wrong choice, which drives you to overthink and avoid risks. This fear might also make you hesitant to delegate decisions, worrying that others might make mistakes. This reluctance can lead to burnout and missed opportunities for your team's growth and development.

Decision fatigue is another challenge you face. The relentless pursuit of the perfect decision can exhaust your cognitive resources, making it harder to make clear, confident choices. For instance, you might spend excessive time debating the best approach to a project, analyzing every possible outcome, which leaves you feeling mentally drained when it's time to decide.

Cognitive biases uniquely affect you as an indecisive overthinker. You might experience confirmation bias, where you seek information supporting your doubts and concerns while ignoring data suggesting a clear path forward. Anchoring bias might make you fixate on initial information or options, unable to move past them even when new, better options are available.

Unmanaged stress is a common problem for you. The pressure to make the right decision can lead you to overcommit and take on too much responsibility, trying to control every aspect of the decision-making process. This relentless pursuit of certainty can result in chronic stress, burnout, and health issues. For example, you might work long hours, continually revisiting decisions and second-guessing yourself, which takes a toll on your well-being.

Despite these challenges, your careful consideration and thoughtful approach are valuable traits. They can lead to well-informed decisions and thorough planning. The key is to find a balance that allows you to make decisions confidently and efficiently. Here are some actions that can help you manage your indecisive tendencies and embrace a more decisive, confident approach:

1. **Set Clear Deadlines:** Establish firm deadlines for making decisions to prevent endless deliberation. Knowing there's a cutoff can help you focus and make timely choices.

2. **Limit Options:** Narrow down your choices to a manageable number. Too many options can be overwhelming, so focus on the most viable ones.

3. **Trust Your Instincts:** Sometimes, your gut feeling can guide you well. Learn to trust your intuition and make decisions based on logic and instinct.

4. **Delegate Decisions:** Empower your team by delegating decisions where appropriate. Trusting others to make choices can relieve your burden and develop their skills.

5. **Embrace Imperfection:** Accept that no decision is perfect and that mistakes are part of the learning process. Making a decision and learning from it is better than making none at all.

6. **Practice Decisiveness:** Make small, low-stakes decisions quickly to build your confidence. Over time, this practice can help you become more decisive with bigger choices.

7. **Focus on Outcomes:** Shift your focus from the decision itself to the desired outcome. What matters is achieving the goal, not necessarily how you get there.

8. **Seek Feedback from Others:** Gather input from trusted colleagues or mentors to gain different perspectives. Their insights can help you feel more confident in your decisions.

9. **Take Breaks to Recharge:** Regular breaks and downtime are crucial for maintaining mental and physical health. Step away from decision-making to recharge and gain clarity.

10. **Celebrate Decisions Made:** Acknowledge and celebrate your decisions, regardless of the outcome. Recognizing your ability to decide can boost your confidence and reduce overthinking.

By implementing these actions, you can manage your indecisive tendencies and embrace a more decisive, confident approach to leadership and life. This balance can lead to more effective decision-making and a healthier, happier you.

As we wrap up this deep dive into self-awareness and growth, let's end with an empowering mantra: "I Cultivate Confident Decisions." This mantra embodies the power and beauty of self-assurance, serving as a beacon of strength and clarity. By embracing these words, you affirm your ability to make decisions confidently and gracefully, acknowledging your wisdom and capability.

To get the most from this mantra, repeat it daily, especially during moments of doubt or indecision. Let it become a cornerstone of your thought process, a reminder that you are capable and resilient. By consistently reinforcing this belief, you align your actions with your aspirations, fostering a mindset of confident decision-making that will guide you through any challenge with poise and certainty.

Lived Experiences: Transformation from Indecisive Overthinker to Confident Leader

"Embrace the courage to decide, for every step taken forward, even with uncertainty, is a step towards progress. Inaction breeds doubt, while action, despite its risks, fosters growth and opportunity." – Jane

Meet Jane, a marketing manager at a mid-sized tech company. Jane is known for her meticulous nature and analytical skills, which made her excellent at identifying potential problems and opportunities. However, her indecisiveness often led to analysis paralysis. She would spend days, sometimes weeks, weighing the pros and cons of every decision, from campaign strategies to budget allocations. This behavior delayed projects and frustrated her team and higher-ups, who needed timely decisions to keep the company moving forward.

One pivotal moment occurred during a major product launch. Jane's hesitation to approve the final marketing plan resulted in a costly miscommunication with a key partner. The partner, expecting prompt approval, had moved forward based on preliminary discussions, only to find out later that significant changes were made at the last minute due to Jane's indecision. This caused confusion and last-minute scrambles and nearly jeopardized the launch. This incident was a wake-up call. Her supervisor discussed the importance of decisive action in leadership roles. Jane realized that her indecisiveness was not just a personal issue but one that affected her entire team and the company's success.

Determined to change, Jane initially found it incredibly difficult to implement new decision-making strategies. She set clear decision criteria, such as defining key objectives and outcomes, but found herself reverting to old habits of overanalyzing each detail. Using tools like pros and cons lists and decision trees helped, but she often got bogged down in the minutiae of each option, second-guessing her conclusions. Each time she tried to decide quickly, a lingering fear of making the wrong choice would creep in, paralyzing her once again.

Jane realized she couldn't do it alone and began to build a support network of colleagues and mentors. This was not an easy task; it meant admitting her struggles to others, which made her feel vulnerable. She discovered that their perspectives and encouragement proved invaluable. They helped her see that no decision is without risk and that taking action was better than stagnating in fear.

Despite this support, Jane faced constant internal battles. She was often up late at night, worrying about her decisions that day and the ones she would need to make the next. Her confidence was fragile, and any negative feedback would send her spiraling back into doubt and overanalysis.

Practicing self-compassion was perhaps the hardest part. Jane had always been her own worst critic, and learning to be kind to herself when mistakes were made felt foreign and uncomfortable. She worked on viewing mistakes as learning opportunities rather than failures, a mindset shift that took time and patience.

Despite the struggles, Jane's transformation was noticeable within weeks. Her team responded positively to her more decisive leadership style. Projects were completed on time, and the overall efficiency of her department improved. The marketing campaigns she spearheaded were more innovative and executed with more and more confidence, leading to increased product visibility and sales. With more success, came more confidence and strength in her decision-making.

Jane's journey from an indecisive overthinker to a confident leader showcases the power of implementing structured decision-making strategies and self-kindness. By setting clear criteria, using decision-making tools, establishing deadlines, and fostering a supportive environment, Jane overcame analysis paralysis. Her story inspires those struggling with indecisiveness, demonstrating that anyone can enhance their decision-making abilities and lead with greater confidence and effectiveness with the right tools and mindset.

Introduction to Reflection Exercise

Journal your responses to the reflection prompts.

Take your time with this exercise. Remember, there is no wrong way to do this. Approach these questions with curiosity and without judgment. Treat it like you are interviewing a close friend. This is an opportunity to gain insight and understanding about your habits and how they impact you and your team.

- **Self-Reflection**: What underlying factors contribute to your difficulty making decisions promptly and confidently?

- **Identify Strengths and Skills:** What strengths and skills have you cultivated that can help you balance your tendency towards indecision? How can you leverage these abilities to take more decisive actions and improve your productivity and leadership?

- **Impact on Team**: How does your indecisiveness affect your team's ability to move forward with projects and feel secure in their roles?

- **Success Memory**: Recall a situation where you made a decisive choice that led to success. What factors helped you make that decision without hesitation?

Self-awareness and insights from reflection are transformative tools for personal and professional growth. Like in any relationship, the more intimately we know ourselves, the closer we become to our authentic selves. This deepened understanding fosters greater confidence, clarity, and purpose. Regularly reflecting on our thoughts, behaviors, and patterns reveals profound truths about who we are and what drives us. This journey towards self-discovery enhances our leadership abilities and aligns our actions with our core values, creating a life of genuine fulfillment and integrity.

7

The Catastrophizer Overthinker

My New Mantra: I Embrace Risk with Optimism

C atastrophizers possess a unique ability to anticipate potential problems, which can be invaluable for risk management and planning. Their keen sense of foresight helps teams prepare for various scenarios, ensuring readiness for challenges that may arise. At the same time, this heightened awareness can sometimes lead to overthinking, where worst-case scenarios dominate their thoughts, resulting in anxiety and hesitation that can impede progress and decision-making.

Imagine being someone who constantly worries about what could go wrong, even when things are going well. You might overanalyze every decision, fearing that the slightest mistake could lead to a catastrophic outcome. This constant vigilance can be exhausting, draining your energy and leaving you feeling stressed and anxious. Does this resonate with you? If so, you are not alone!

As a Catastrophizer, your overthinking might be rooted in past ex-periences where unexpected problems arose, leading you always to anticipate the worst. This mindset can make you highly cautious and detail-oriented as you strive to foresee and prevent potential issues. While this can result in thorough planning, it can cause significant stress and delays.

Your tendency to focus on negative outcomes can impact those around you. For instance, your team might pick up on your anxiety, leading to a tense and uncertain work environment. While your caution can help avoid some pitfalls, it can also stifle creativity and innovation, as fear of failure prevents you from taking necessary risks.

Analysis paralysis is a common challenge for you. You might get stuck in endless loops of "what if" scenarios, unable to decide for fear of making the wrong one. This indecisiveness can frustrate your team, who may be ready to move forward while you're still considering all possible negative outcomes.

Fear of failure is a significant driver of your overthinking. You might worry excessively about disappointing others or facing consequences if things don't go as planned. This fear can lead you to avoid taking action altogether, missing out on opportunities for growth and success.

Decision fatigue is another hurdle you face. Constantly weighing potential risks and negative outcomes can be mentally exhausting, leaving you drained when making important decisions. For example, you might spend hours analyzing the pros and cons of a business proposal, only to feel too exhausted to make a confident choice.

Cognitive biases play a significant role in your overthinking. You might be prone to negativity bias, focusing more on potential problems than possible positive outcomes. This can lead to a skewed perspective, where the risks seem much greater than they are. Additionally, confirmation bias might make you seek out information that supports your fears, reinforcing your catastrophic thinking.

Unmanaged stress is a constant companion for you as a Catastrophizer. The habit of always expecting the worst can lead to chronic stress, affecting your health and well-being. You might find yourself constantly tense, with difficulty relaxing and enjoying the present moment.

Despite these challenges, your ability to foresee potential problems is valuable. It can help you prepare for and mitigate risks, leading to more resilient planning and execution. The key is to balance this with a more optimistic and realistic outlook. Here are some actions to help you manage your catastrophic thinking and embrace a healthier, more proactive approach:

1. **Challenge Negative Thoughts:** When you catch yourself spiraling into worst-case scenarios, take a moment to question the likelihood of these outcomes. Replace catastrophic thoughts with more balanced, realistic ones.

2. **Practice Mindfulness:** Mindfulness techniques, such as meditation or deep breathing, can help calm your mind and reduce anxiety. This practice encourages you to stay present rather than worrying about future disasters.

3. **Create a Structured Plan:** Develop a clear, step-by-step plan for your tasks and goals. A structured approach can

reduce feelings of overwhelm and provide a clear path forward, minimizing the space for catastrophic thinking.

4. **Focus on What You Can Control:** Identify what aspects of a situation you can influence and take proactive steps in those areas. Let go of worries about things beyond your control.

5. **Seek Perspective from Others:** Talk to trusted colleagues or friends about your concerns. They can provide alternative viewpoints and help you see the situation more clearly.

6. **Limit Information Overload:** Too much information can fuel your catastrophic thinking. Be selective about the sources you consult and focus on credible, balanced information.

7. **Take Small Steps Forward:** Break larger tasks into smaller, manageable steps. This approach reduces the feeling of being overwhelmed and makes progress more achievable.

8. **Celebrate Small Wins:** Acknowledge and celebrate small achievements along the way. This positive reinforcement can boost your confidence and counterbalance your tendency to focus on negatives.

9. **Develop a Contingency Plan:** A backup plan can ease your anxiety about potential problems. Knowing you have a strategy if things go wrong can provide peace of mind.

10. **Seek Professional Support:** If catastrophic thinking significantly impacts your daily life, consider seeking help from a therapist or counselor. Professional guidance can provide effective strategies for managing anxiety and overthinking.

By implementing these actions, you can harness your ability to foresee potential challenges while maintaining a balanced and proactive mindset. This approach can lead to more confident decision-making, reduced stress, and a healthier, happier you.

As we wrap up this deep dive into self-awareness and growth, let's end with an empowering mantra: "I Embrace Risk with Optimism." This mantra encapsulates the courage to face uncertainty with a positive outlook, transforming potential fears into opportunities for growth. The power and beauty of this mantra lie in its ability to shift your mindset, fostering resilience and encouraging a proactive approach to life's challenges.

Understanding and addressing the unique challenges Catastrophizer leaders face can transform the decision-making approach. More effective leadership can be achieved by refocusing on positive outcomes, managing decision fatigue, developing realistic risk assessments, and alleviating cognitive overload. These strategies help overcome overthinking, enabling successful guidance of teams and fostering a healthier, more productive work environment.

Lived Experiences: Transformation from Catastrophizer to Effective Leader

"Embrace the unknown with courage, for every step forward is a victory over fear." – Will

Meet Will, a senior logistics manager at a manufacturing company. Will is an accomplished senior logistics manager at a leading manufacturing company. He has a knack for identifying potential risks in the supply chain, making him a valuable asset to his team. However, his tendency to focus excessively on what could go wrong often led to significant delays in decision-making. Will's constant worry about potential disasters caused him to overanalyze every aspect of the logistics operations, resulting in stalled projects and growing frustration among his team.

The tipping point came during the implementation of a new inventory management system. Will's incessant focus on potential failures caused numerous delays, pushing the project timeline back by months. His team, eager to move forward, grew increasingly demoralized as Will's indecision continually stalled their efforts. The company started losing its competitive edge as customers faced delays and disruptions. Realizing the negative impact of his catastrophic thinking, Will knew he had to change his approach.

Determined to overcome his tendencies, Will started working with a leadership coach. There, he learned tools to help shift his mindset. One of the first strategies Will adopted was positive visualization. He began each day by envisioning successful outcomes for his projects rather than dwelling on potential problems. This practice helped him build confidence and reduce his anxiety about making decisions.

Will participated in risk management training to gain a more realistic perspective on risks. He learned structured techniques to assess the actual likelihood and impact of potential issues, which helped him differentiate between real risks and imagined catastrophes. This training was crucial in helping Will ground his fears in reality.

Will also implemented strict time limits for making decisions. By setting specific deadlines, he avoided getting caught in endless loops of overthinking. Although challenging initially, this practice forced him to make timely decisions and keep projects moving forward. Additionally, he categorized decisions into high-stakes and low-stakes, focusing his mental energy on the most critical issues.

Seeking further support, Will reached out to a senior mentor within the company. This mentor provided valuable insights and challenged Will's catastrophic thinking, helping him see situations more clearly and make balanced decisions.

The changes Will made had a profound impact. Projects began to progress more smoothly, and team morale improved significantly. The new inventory management system, once plagued by delays, was finally implemented successfully and received positive feedback from both the team and customers. The company regained its competitive edge, and Will's team felt more empowered and confident under his leadership.

Will's journey from a Catastrophizer overthinker to an effective leader highlights the power of targeted strategies in overcoming deep-seated fears. By practicing positive visualization, engaging in risk management training, setting time limits for decisions, and seeking mentorship, Will was able to transform his approach to leadership. His story demonstrates that Catastrophizer leaders can break free from overthinking, lead their teams more effectively, and create a more positive and productive work environment with the right tools and mindset.

————◆◇◆————

Introduction to Reflection Exercise

Journal your responses to the reflection prompts.

Take your time with this exercise. Remember, there is no wrong way to do this. Approach these questions with curiosity and without judgment. Treat it like you are interviewing a close friend. This is an opportunity to gain insight and understanding about your habits and how they impact you and your team.

- **Self-Reflection**: What past experiences or outcomes have contributed to your tendency to focus on worst-case scenarios?

- **Identify Strengths and Skills:** What strengths and skills have you cultivated that can help you balance your tendency to focus on worst-case scenarios? How can you leverage these abilities to foster a more optimistic and realistic approach in your leadership?

- **Impact on Team**: How does your focus on potential risks impact your team's willingness to innovate and take calculated risks?

- **Success Memory**: Recall a time when you confidently made a decision that led to a positive result. How did you overcome your fears in that situation?

Self-awareness and insights from reflection are transformative tools for personal and professional growth. Like in any relationship, the more intimately we know ourselves, the closer we become to our authentic selves. This deepened understanding fosters greater confidence, clarity, and purpose. Regularly reflecting on our thoughts, behaviors, and patterns reveals profound truths about who we are and what drives us. This journey towards self-discovery enhances our leadership abilities and aligns our actions with our core values, creating a life of genuine fulfillment and integrity.

8

The Procrastinator Overthinker

My New Mantra: I Transform Deliberation into Action

Procrastinators have a unique ability to prioritize tasks based on urgency, often leading to effective time management when deadlines loom. This knack for handling pressure ensures they can deliver quality work under tight constraints, impressing those around them with their ability to perform in crunch time. At the same time, this tendency to delay action can sometimes result in last-minute stress and rushed decisions, contributing to overthinking and anxiety. By understanding and addressing these patterns, procrastinators can find a balance between timely action and maintaining their composure, reducing the negative impacts of overthinking.

Imagine being someone who often delays starting projects, waiting until the pressure of a looming deadline forces action. This can lead to a rush to complete tasks, often resulting in subpar outcomes and increased stress. The fear of not performing perfectly or making mistakes can cause you to avoid tasks altogether, leading to a backlog of work and mounting anxiety. Does this resonate with you? If so, you are not alone!

As a procrastinator, your overthinking might stem from past experiences where taking action led to criticism or failure. You might develop a habit of overanalyzing every detail to avoid these out-comes, but this can paralyze you and prevent progress. Personal insecurities or a professional environment emphasizing perfection might also contribute to your tendency to procrastinate.

This habit can significantly impact your work and those around you. On one hand, your thoroughness and desire to avoid mistakes can lead to careful planning and attention to detail. On the other hand, delays in decision-making and task completion can frustrate team members, lead to missed opportunities, and create a stressful work environment. Your hesitation can slow progress and impact team morale, as colleagues might feel the pressure of last-minute rushes or the burden of picking up the slack.

Recognizing the dynamics of procrastination starts with under-standing the struggle with starting tasks. You might endlessly plan and prepare, seeking the perfect moment to begin, which often never comes. Fear of failure is a significant factor, as the possibility of not meeting high standards or making mistakes can make starting a task seem daunting. This fear can drive you to put off tasks, hoping that you will be better equipped to handle them in the future.

Decision fatigue is another challenge. The constant overthinking and delaying decisions can exhaust your cognitive resources, mak-ing it even harder to start or complete tasks. For example, you might spend excessive time weighing the pros and cons of every possible action, leading to mental exhaustion and indecision. You may feel too drained to perform effectively when it's finally time to act.

Cognitive biases also play a role in procrastination. Confirmation bias might lead you to seek out information that justifies delaying tasks, while anchoring bias can cause you to fixate on a project's initial overwhelming scope, making it hard to break it down into manageable steps. This can create a vicious cycle where the more you delay, the more daunting the task appears, reinforcing your procrastination habit.

Unmanaged stress is a common problem for procrastinators. The pressure of impending deadlines and the guilt of delayed tasks can lead to chronic stress and burnout. You might work long hours at the last minute, trying to complete tasks under pressure, which can ultimately take a toll on your well-being and result in lower-quality work.

Despite these challenges, your meticulous attention to detail and reflective nature are valuable traits. They can lead to well-informed decisions and thorough planning. The key is to find a balance that allows you to take action and move forward effectively. Here are some strategies that can help you manage your procrastination tendencies and embrace a more proactive, confident approach:

1. **Break Tasks into Smaller Steps:** Divide large projects into smaller, more manageable tasks to make starting less daunting.

2. **Set Specific Deadlines:** Establish clear, realistic deadlines for each task to create a sense of urgency and accountability.

3. **Prioritize Tasks:** To avoid feeling overwhelmed, focus on the most important tasks first and tackle them one at a

time.

4. **Limit Planning Time:** Allocate a specific amount of time for planning and stick to it to avoid getting stuck in endless preparation.

5. **Use a Timer:** Work in short, focused bursts using a timer to maintain concentration and momentum.

6. **Practice Self-Compassion:** Be kind to yourself and recognize that perfection is unrealistic. Allow yourself to make mistakes and learn from them.

7. **Seek Accountability:** Share your goals with a friend or colleague who can help keep you on track and provide support.

8. **Create a Positive Work Environment:** Minimize distractions and create a workspace that encourages focus and productivity.

9. **Reward Progress:** Celebrate small achievements to stay motivated and build momentum.

10. **Reflect on Successes:** Regularly review and reflect on past successes to remind yourself of your capabilities and reduce the fear of failure.

By implementing these actions, you can manage your procrastination and turn overthinking into a productive force. This balance can lead to more consistent progress, reduced stress, and a healthier approach to achieving your goals.

As we wrap up this deep dive into self-awareness and growth, let's end with an empowering mantra: "I Transform Deliberation into Action." This mantra encapsulates the essence of turning thoughtful consideration into decisive movement, a vital shift for any leader or individual seeking growth. The power and beauty of this mantra lie in its simplicity and profound impact. By repeating it daily, especially in moments of hesitation, reinforces the belief that thoughtful deliberation is a strength that propels forward rather than holding back.

To get the most from this mantra, integrate it into your morning routine, meditate on it during quiet moments, and remind yourself of it whenever facing a challenging decision. Embrace this mantra as a guiding light, transforming careful thought into purposeful action, and watch as it cultivates confidence, clarity, and momentum in your life.

Lived Experiences: Transformation from Procrastinator Overthinker to Strategic Decision-Maker

"Procrastination is the thief of options. Start now, take small steps, and trust that progress, not perfection, will lead you to success." – Lori

Meet Lori, a senior trainer in the human resources department at a well-established consumer goods company. Lori is renowned for her innovative training programs and deep understanding of employee development. However, her tendency to overthink and procrastinate on decisions often led to missed deadlines and stressed-out trainees. Lori's reluctance to make quick decisions, fueled by a fear of making mistakes, resulted in analysis paralysis, hindering the effectiveness of her training sessions.

The breaking point came during the planning of a major training initiative for the holiday season. Lori's indecision about the training strategy caused significant delays. As a result, the program missed the critical preparation period, and the company lost a substantial amount of potential productivity improvement. The CEO, recognizing Lori's talent but concerned about her decision-making habits, arranged a meeting to discuss the importance of timely and strategic decisions.

Determined to change, Lori began by setting clear deadlines for her decisions. Initially, she struggled with letting go of her need for exhaustive information. Using tools like decision trees and pros and cons lists helped, but Lori often found herself bogged down in the details, unable to commit.

Lori also tried to break down larger tasks into smaller, more manageable steps. This was challenging for her as she was accustomed to tackling big projects all at once. Despite setting incremental goals, Lori was overwhelmed by the sheer volume of tasks. She also struggled to maintain accountability, even though she scheduled regular check-ins with a mentor. Admitting when she was behind was hard, and old habits of delaying decisions crept in.

Despite these initial hurdles, Lori persisted. She started implementing the two-minute rule, addressing small decisions immediately instead of letting them accumulate. This small change began to improve her daily workflow significantly. Additionally, Lori set specific times during the day dedicated to decision-making, which helped her stay focused and reduce mental fatigue.

Building a strong support network was crucial for Lori. Her mentor provided valuable perspective and encouragement. Regular check-ins helped her stay accountable and recognize her progress, even when it was slow. Lori also faced personal struggles with self-doubt and fear of failure, often waking up in the middle of the night worrying about pending decisions. Understanding the costs of delay and the benefits of proactive decision-making became an essential part of her transformation.

Lori learned to identify signs of decision fatigue, such as irritability and avoidance behavior. Implementing strategies to manage her energy better was vital. She ensured she rested well and maintained a healthy work-life balance, but breaking old habits of overworking and stressing about decisions was a constant struggle. Delegating some decision-making responsibilities to her team helped reduce her cognitive load and empowered her colleagues—though, initially, Lori found it hard to trust others with important decisions.

Within a few months, Lori's transformation was evident. Her improved decisiveness led to higher efficiency and morale within her team. Training programs were completed on time, and the overall productivity of her assigned departments increased. One notable success was the execution of a new leadership training program. Lori's proactive decision-making and clear guidance led to a smooth rollout, impressive participant feedback, and improved leadership skills across the company.

This success boosted the company's employee performance metrics and earned Lori recognition and praise from her peers and superiors. Her ability to make confident, strategic decisions ultimately paid off.

Lori's journey from a procrastinator overthinker to a strategic de-cision-maker highlights the power of structured decision-making strategies. By setting clear deadlines, using decision-making tools, breaking tasks into manageable steps, and fostering accountabil-ity, Lori overcame her tendency to procrastinate. Her story inspires other leaders struggling with similar issues, demonstrating that anyone can enhance their decision-making abilities and lead with greater confidence and effectiveness with the right tools and mindset.

Introduction to Reflection Exercise

Journal your responses to the reflection prompts.

Take your time with this exercise. Remember, there is no wrong way to do this. Approach these questions with curiosity and with-out judgment. Treat it like you are interviewing a close friend. This is an opportunity to gain insight and understanding about your habits and how they impact you and your team.

- **Self-Reflection**: What fears or beliefs lead you to delay decision-making and action?

- **Identify Strengths and Skills:** What strengths and skills have you cultivated that can help you balance your ten-dency to procrastinate? How can you leverage these abil-ities to take more decisive actions and improve your pro-ductivity and leadership?

- **Impact on Team**: How do your procrastination habits influence your team's stress levels and ability to meet deadlines effectively?

- **Success Memory**: Think of a time when you took prompt action that resulted in success. What did you learn about the benefits of timely decision-making from that experience?

Self-awareness and insights from reflection are transformative tools for personal and professional growth. Like in any relationship, the more intimately we know ourselves, the closer we become to our authentic selves. This deepened understanding fosters greater confidence, clarity, and purpose. Regularly reflecting on our thoughts, behaviors, and patterns reveals profound truths about who we are and what drives us. This journey towards self-discovery enhances our leadership abilities and aligns actions with our core values, creating a life of genuine fulfillment and integrity.

Unlock the Power of Generosity

"Helping one person might not change the whole world, but it could change the world for one person." - Unknown

Make a Difference with Your Review

Most people do, in fact, judge a book by its cover (and its reviews).

So here's my ask on behalf of struggling leaders you've never met: Please help those leaders by leaving this book a review. Your gift costs no money and takes less than 60 seconds to make real, but it can change a fellow leader's life forever.

Scan the QR code to leave your review:

https://www.amazon.com/dp/196389507

Thank you from the bottom of my heart. Now, back to our regularly scheduled programming.

With gratitude, Bonnie

9

Foundational Solutions for Overthinking

"Self-care is giving the world the best of you, instead of what's left of you." – Katie Reed

T o be a healthy, balanced leader, it's important to start by focusing on individual well-being. The more a leader invests in personal needs and happiness, the more there is to give to the world. Research consistently shows that leaders prioritizing their health and well-being positively influence their teams' overall health and performance. Investing in wellness and balance elevates leadership to the next level.

As the journey to address overthinking continues, it's time to shift focus from reactive strategies to foundational solutions. These solutions provide preventative measures designed to heal overthinking at its core, fostering a sense of balance, empowerment, and agility. By integrating these practices into daily life, a solid foundation can be built that prevents overthinking and promotes overall mental well-being.

This chapter delves into essential techniques and lifestyle adjustments that help cultivate a resilient mindset, enabling navigating life's challenges with grace and confidence. Scientific studies have shown that individuals who maintain a healthy lifestyle, manage stress effectively, and practice self-care create a spreading influence, leading to healthier, more engaged, and more productive team members.

Through these foundational strategies, a more harmonious and empowered existence can be created, reducing the likelihood of overthinking and enhancing the ability to respond to situations with clarity and purpose. Transformative approaches and how to incorporate them into routines for lasting impact will be explored. These practices benefit individuals and strengthen leadership capabilities, ultimately contributing to the success and cohesion of teams. Embracing these changes, supported by scientific evidence, unlocks the potential for a balanced and impactful life.

Mindfulness and Meditation

Mindfulness and meditation are powerful tools that enhance self-awareness, reduce stress, and improve emotional regulation. Whether new to these practices or having heard about them but never tried, this section guides through the basics in a clear and easy-to-follow manner.

Mindfulness is the practice of being fully present and engaged in the moment. It means paying attention to thoughts, feelings, and sensations without judgment. Think of it as tuning into the here and now instead of being caught up in worries about the past or future. Neuroscientifically, mindfulness has increased the density of gray matter in brain regions linked to learning, memory, emotion regulation, and perspective-taking.

Meditation is a practice where techniques like focusing the mind on a particular object, thought, or activity are used to train attention and awareness. It's a way to achieve a mentally clear and emotionally calm state. Research has demonstrated that regular meditation practice can alter the brain's structure and function, improving areas associated with attention, empathy, and stress.

Numerous neuroscience studies support the idea that mindfulness and meditation can lead to significant changes in the brain. Regular practice has increased gray matter in the hippocampus, a region important for learning, memory, and emotional regulation. Additionally, the amygdala, the brain's stress and fear center, shows reduced activity in regularly meditating people. This reduction correlates with lower stress levels and better emotional regulation.

Meditation also enhances the connectivity between brain regions involved in attention and self-awareness, such as the prefrontal cortex, which is crucial for planning, decision-making, and moderating social behavior. Moreover, studies have found that the cortical regions related to sensory processing and attention become thicker with regular meditation, suggesting improved cognitive functions and heightened sensory awareness.

By incorporating mindfulness and meditation into a daily routine, numerous benefits that enhance overall well-being can be experienced. Practicing mindfulness and meditation helps one better understand oneself by making one more aware of thoughts and feelings, leading to enhanced self-awareness. These practices also calm the mind, aiding in more effective stress management and reducing stress levels. Additionally, mindfulness and meditation help respond to emotions with greater clarity and calmness, improving emotional regulation. Regular practice improves attention span and concentration, improving focus and concentration. Many find that mindfulness and meditation contribute to greater well-being and increased happiness.

Something To Try: Getting Started with Mindfulness

No special equipment or a lot of time is needed to start practicing mindfulness. Here are some simple steps to get started:

Mindful Movement: Breezing

Breezing is a soothing technique often instinctively used by children. It is a powerful method for releasing energy, providing comfort, and promoting calmness in the mind, body, and spirit. To practice breezing, follow these steps:

1. Stand with feet spread apart for a stable base.

2. Allow arms to hang loosely by your sides. Begin to gently swing them back and forth, letting them naturally rise and fall with each twisting movement.

3. Focus on breathing, allowing natural breaths.

4. After a few minutes of breezing, pause to feel the calm, soothing relaxation sweep through the mind and body.

5. This process of gentle, rhythmic arm-swinging combined with breathing helps in energy release and achieving relaxation and balance.

Simple Mindfulness Exercise: 5-4-3-2-1 Grounding Technique

The 5-4-3-2-1 grounding technique is a quick and effective way to bring attention to the present moment. Here's how to do it:

1. Find a Comfortable Position: Sit or stand comfortably.

2. Take Deep Breaths: Start relaxing with a few deep breaths.

3. Identify Five Things You Can See: Notice anything in the surroundings, from a picture on the wall to a piece of furniture.

4. Identify Four Things You Can Touch: Feel the texture of clothing, the surface of a table, or anything else within reach.

5. Identify Three Things You Can Hear: Pay attention to surrounding sounds, such as the hum of a computer, chirping birds, or distant traffic.

6. Identify Two Things You Can Smell: Take a deep breath and notice two scents. This could be soap, fresh air, or anything else.

7. Identify One Thing You Can Taste: It could be the lingering taste of the last meal or a sip of water.

8. Take a Final Deep Breath: After completing the steps, take a final deep breath and notice feeling more grounded and present.

Starting Meditation

Meditation can seem daunting at first, but it's very simple. Here's a basic meditation practice to get started:

1. Find a Quiet Place: Choose a quiet spot to sit comfortably without being disturbed.

2. Set a Timer: Start with just 5 minutes. Gradually increase the time as comfort grows.

3. Sit Comfortably: Sit in a chair or on the floor with a straight back and hands resting on knees.

4. Focus on Your Breath: Close your eyes and focus on breathing. Notice the sensation of the air entering and leaving the nostrils.

5. Return to Your Breath: When the mind wanders, gently bring attention back to the breath.

6. End Gently: When the timer goes off, slowly open your eyes and notice how you feel.

Consistency is key to positive change. When striving for consistent practice, being patient with yourself is essential. It's normal for the mind to wander; the key is gently bringing your focus back without judgment. Practicing daily is crucial, as consistency is more important than duration. Even a few minutes each day can make a significant difference. Using guided meditations from apps and online resources can be very helpful, especially for beginners. Additionally, creating a routine by practicing at the same time each day, such as in the morning or evening, can help build a lasting habit.

Mindfulness and meditation are wonderful practices that can bring more peace, clarity, and joy into life. By starting with these simple steps, you can experience the benefits. Remember, there's no right or wrong way to practice—the key is to be consistent and kind to yourself while exploring these new techniques.

Quality Sleep

If you're looking for a single practice to significantly and rapidly impact well-being, prioritizing mindful sleep should be at the top of the list. Restorative sleep is crucial for mental health, allowing the brain to process daily events, consolidate memories, and rejuvenate. Without enough quality sleep, the brain struggles to function optimally, leading to increased anxiety, diminished concentration, and rampant overthinking. By ensuring you get deep, uninterrupted sleep, you can significantly reduce the cycle of repetitive and unproductive thinking patterns.

Quality sleep means getting 7-9 hours of uninterrupted, restful sleep each night. Think of sleep as a nightly reset button for your body and brain, allowing you to function at your best every day.

Getting enough quality sleep offers numerous benefits, among the most significant being improved memory and concentration. When you sleep well, your brain processes and stores memories more effectively, helping you learn and remember things better. Good sleep also reduces stress and improves overall mood, making you feel happier and more relaxed.

Another benefit is enhanced physical health, as sleep supports the immune system, reduces inflammation, and helps regulate vital functions like blood pressure. Additionally, quality sleep leaves you feeling refreshed and energetic, ready to tackle the day. Proper sleep also helps regulate hormones that control hunger, reducing the risk of overeating and weight gain.

When you consistently don't get enough sleep, it can seriously affect your health and well-being. One immediate effect is decreased cognitive function; lack of sleep impairs your ability to think clearly, concentrate, and make decisions. This mental fog can hinder your performance in daily activities and reduce overall productivity.

Moreover, poor sleep is linked to an increased risk of developing chronic conditions such as heart disease, diabetes, Alzheimer's disease, and obesity. Your body needs adequate rest to regulate critical functions; without it, these health risks rise significantly. Insufficient sleep also weakens the immune system, compromising your ability to fight off infections and making you more susceptible to illnesses.

Emotionally, sleep deprivation can lead to instability, manifesting as irritability, mood swings, and even depression. These emotional disturbances can strain your relationships and diminish your mental health. Furthermore, chronic sleep deprivation results in persistent physical fatigue, sapping your energy and reducing your overall quality of life. In sum, consistently not getting enough sleep can severely impact your physical and mental well-being.

Quality sleep requires a nightly routine of rejuvenating rest. Many people believe they can catch up on lost sleep by sleeping more on weekends. However, this is a myth. Consistently shortchanging your sleep during the week cannot be fully compensated by extra sleep on weekends. This erratic sleep pattern can actually disrupt your natural rhythm, making it even harder to get regular quality sleep. The key is to maintain a regular sleep schedule every day.

Something To Try: Achieve Quality Sleep

- **Stick to a Schedule:** Go to bed and wake up at the same time every day, even on weekends. This helps regulate your body's internal clock.

- **Create a Relaxing Bedtime Routine:** Before bed, engage in calming activities like reading, listening to soothing music, or taking a warm bath.

- **Limit Exposure to Electronics:** Keep electronic devices like phones, tablets, and laptops away from your bed. The blue light emitted by these screens can interfere with your body's production of melatonin, a hormone that regulates sleep.

- **Avoid Stimulants Before Bed:** Avoid consuming caffeine or heavy meals close to bedtime. These can disrupt your sleep cycle.

- **Make Your Sleep Environment Comfortable:** Ensure your bedroom is dark, quiet, and cool. Use a comfortable mattress and pillows.

Creating a restful sleep environment is essential for overall well-being, and a key aspect of this is managing the presence of electronic devices near your bed. Keeping electronic devices away from your head while you sleep is crucial for several reasons.

Firstly, reducing exposure to blue light is essential. The blue light emitted by screens can trick your brain into thinking it's daytime, making it harder to fall asleep. By keeping devices away, you can help maintain your natural sleep cycle and improve the quality of your rest.

Secondly, minimizing distractions is important for uninterrupted sleep. Notifications and alerts from electronic devices can disrupt sleep, causing you to wake up throughout the night. Ensuring your devices are out of reach can help you stay asleep and wake up feeling refreshed.

Lowering exposure to electromagnetic radiation is also a good precaution for better sleep. While research is ongoing, reducing the electromagnetic radiation from devices near your head is considered beneficial for maintaining a healthy sleep environment.

Furthermore, using your phone as an alarm clock is not a good practice. Keeping your phone on silent and placing it in a drawer or another room can further reduce the temptation to check it at night, allowing you to enjoy a more restful sleep. This practice helps reduce blue light exposure and electromagnetic radiation and eliminates potential sleep disruptions from notifications and alerts. Creating a device-free sleep zone promotes a healthier and more restorative sleep environment.

Quality sleep is not a luxury; it's a necessity for overall health and well-being. Prioritizing good sleep habits will make you more energized, focused, and happier. Remember, getting 7-9 hours of quality sleep each night is one of the best things you can do for your body and mind.

Journaling

Finding mental and emotional clarity can often feel like an elusive goal in the whirlwind of daily life. Maintaining balance and regulation may seem challenging with constant thoughts, responsibilities, and emotions. However, there is a simple yet profoundly effective tool that can serve as an anchor in the storm: journaling.

Journaling is more than just writing down your thoughts; it's a powerful practice that fosters self-awareness, clarity, and emotional regulation. Putting pen to paper creates a tangible connection between your mind and your experiences, allowing for a deeper understanding and processing of your inner world.

When your mind is cluttered with thoughts, worries, and to-do lists, it can be difficult to think clearly. Journaling acts as a mental decluttering process. By writing down your thoughts, you externalize them, creating space in your mind for clearer thinking. This process helps you organize your thoughts by sorting through jumbled ideas and bringing order and coherence to them. It also aids in prioritizing tasks, helping you decide what needs immediate attention and what can be scheduled for later. Moreover, journaling facilitates decision-making by weighing pros and cons, considering different perspectives, and making more informed choices.

Emotions can be overwhelming, and if left unchecked, they can lead to stress and imbalance. Journaling is an emotional release valve, providing a safe space to express and explore your feelings. It aids in processing emotions by helping you understand and reduce their intensity and impact. Regular journaling can reveal emotional patterns and triggers, helping you anticipate and manage them better.

Consistent journaling encourages self-reflection, which is key to emotional regulation. By reflecting on your experiences and reactions, you can better understand yourself and your emotional responses. This self-awareness leads to improved self-control, as understanding your emotional triggers allows you to develop strategies for managing them. It also enhances stress management, as reflecting on stressful events and how you handled them helps build resilience and better coping mechanisms for future stressors. Ultimately, regular reflection promotes personal growth by highlighting areas for improvement and celebrating your progress.

Types of Journaling

There are various journaling techniques you can explore to find what resonates best with you:

- **Stream of Consciousness:** Write continuously without worrying about grammar or structure. This free-flowing style helps in unloading thoughts and emotions.

- **Gratitude Journal:** Focus on the positive by writing down things you are grateful for each day. This practice enhances your mood and overall outlook on life.

- **Reflection Journal:** Reflect on your day, noting what went well, what didn't, and what you learned. This helps in understanding your experiences and emotions.

- **Prompt Journaling:** Use prompts to guide your writing. Prompts can range from "What am I feeling right now?" to "What are my goals for the next month?" This approach can help you explore specific areas of your life more deeply.

- **Bullet Journal:** Combine planning and journaling by using bullet points to organize your thoughts, tasks, and reflections. This method is great for those who prefer a structured approach.

Something To Try: Start a Journaling Practice

Starting a journaling practice is simple, but consistency is key. Here are some tips to help you get started:

- **Set a Routine:** Choose a specific time each day for journaling. Whether it's first thing in the morning or before bed, consistency helps build the habit.

- **Find a Comfortable Space:** Create a quiet and comfortable space for journaling. This will help you focus and relax as you write.

- **Be Honest:** Write honestly and openly. Your journal is a judgment-free zone, so don't hold back.

- **Keep It Simple:** Don't worry about writing perfectly. The goal is to express yourself, not to create a masterpiece.

- **Use Prompts if Stuck:** If you're unsure what to write about, use prompts to get started. There are many prompt ideas available online to inspire you.

Journaling is a powerful tool for achieving mental and emotional clarity, balance, and regulation. When you dedicate time to this practice, you give yourself the space to explore your thoughts and emotions, leading to greater self-awareness and well-being. The journey of journaling is personal and unique to each individual. Embrace it with an open heart and mind, allowing the words to guide you toward a more balanced and fulfilled life.

Physical Activity

Physical activity is more than just a way to stay fit; it's vital to holistic well-being. Regular exercise, whether walking, jogging, yoga, or strength training, maintains physical health and significantly boosts mental well-being. Let's dive into the profound benefits of physical activity, explore different types of exercises, and see how to integrate them into daily routines for a balanced life.

The benefits of physical activity are extensive and multifaceted. For physical health, regular exercise strengthens the heart and improves circulation, significantly reducing the risk of cardiovascular diseases. Activities like jogging, brisk walking, and cycling are excellent for maintaining heart health. Strength training and yoga enhance muscle strength, flexibility, and joint health, which are essential for maintaining posture, preventing injuries, and improving overall physical performance.

Additionally, engaging in physical activity helps with mental well-being. Physical activity triggers the release of endorphins, often called the "feel-good" hormones. These endorphins help reduce stress, anxiety, and depression, promoting a sense of well-being. Regular exercise can also help regulate sleep patterns, leading to better quality sleep, which is essential for mental clarity, emotional stability, and overall health.

Moreover, physical activity has been shown to improve memory, attention, and cognitive function by stimulating the growth of new brain cells and enhancing brain plasticity. Achieving fitness goals and regular exercise can boost self-confidence and self-esteem, contributing to a positive self-image.

Integrating physical activity into a daily routine doesn't have to be daunting or overly strenuous. Emphasizing fun and enjoyment over intense training can make exercise a sustainable and delightful part of life. When physical activity is enjoyable, it becomes something to look forward to rather than a chore. This positive association increases the likelihood of consistency, which is crucial for long-term health benefits.

Engaging in enjoyable activities also reduces the risk of burnout and injury. By choosing loved activities, such as dancing, hiking, playing a sport, or even gardening, it's possible to naturally incorporate more movement into life without the pressure of "training hard." This approach ensures that physical activity remains a joyful and integral part of a holistic well-being journey.

Something To Try: Integrate Daily Physical Activity

- **Set Realistic Goals:** Start with achievable goals and gradually increase the intensity and duration of workouts. This approach helps maintain motivation and prevent burnout.

- **Create a Schedule:** Dedicate specific times for physical activity in your daily routine. Consistency is key to reaping the benefits of exercise.

- **Find Activities You Enjoy:** Choose exercises that are enjoyable and fulfilling. Whether dancing, swimming, or hiking, engaging in activities you love will make it easier to stick to a routine.

- **Incorporate Variety:** Mix different types of exercises to keep your routine interesting and work different muscle groups. This prevents monotony and promotes overall fitness.

- **Listen to Your Body:** Pay attention to your body's signals and avoid overexertion. Rest and recovery are essential components of a balanced fitness regimen.

- **Seek Support:** To stay motivated and accountable, join a fitness group, partner with a friend, or hire a personal trainer.

Embracing physical activity is a powerful step towards achieving holistic well-being and helps resolve overthinking. By integrating regular exercise into daily routines, a myriad of physical and mental health benefits can be enjoyed. Whether it's a peaceful walk in the park, an invigorating jog, a calming yoga session, or a strength training workout, each form of physical activity contributes to a healthier, happier, and more balanced life. Remember, the journey to well-being is a marathon, not a sprint. Start today, stay consistent, and watch your body and mind transform.

Positive Relationships

Positive relationships are fundamental to well-being and success. The people surrounding you profoundly impact your mood, motivation, and overall life satisfaction. Cultivating and maintaining positive relationships with family, friends, and colleagues enriches life, providing a support system that uplifts and encourages. Let's delve into the importance of these relationships and explore strategies for nurturing and sustaining them.

Humans are inherently social beings. From the earliest stages of life, interactions shape experiences and influence development. Positive relationships provide emotional support, reduce stress, and contribute to a sense of belonging. They enhance mental and physical health, foster personal growth, and increase resilience in facing challenges. On the other hand, negative or toxic relationships can drain energy, diminish self-esteem, and hinder progress.

Maintaining mutual respect and honesty with the people in your life is essential. Addressing conflicts openly and constructively and always striving to treat others with kindness and respect can help relationships thrive and bring immense joy and fulfillment to life.

Something To Try: Uplifting Relationships

The people you surround yourself with significantly influence your mindset and outlook on life. Here are some tips for creating a supportive and uplifting social network:

- **Choose Wisely:** Be selective about the people you spend the most time with. Surround yourself with individuals who inspire, motivate, and uplift you. Seek out those who share your values and encourage your growth.

- **Set Boundaries:** Establish and maintain healthy boundaries to protect yourself from negative influences and toxic relationships that drain your energy and dampen your spirit.

- **Be Uplifting:** Strive to be an uplifting presence in others' lives. Offer support, encouragement, and positivity. Being a source of light for others attracts similar energy into your own life.

- **Engage in Communities:** Participate in communities and groups that align with your interests and values. Whether it's a hobby group, a professional association, or a volunteer organization, being part of a community fosters a sense of belonging and connection.

Cultivating and maintaining positive relationships with family, friends, and colleagues is essential for a fulfilling and balanced life. By investing time and effort into these connections, practicing open communication, and surrounding yourself with supportive and uplifting people, you create a network of love and support that sustains through life's ups and downs. This network provides emotional support and helps resolve overthinking by offering different perspectives and reassuring moments of doubt. The quality of relationships profoundly impacts happiness and well-being, so nurture them with care, respect, and gratitude.

Personal Development

In today's fast-paced world, continuous learning and personal development aren't just luxuries but essential to maintaining mental and emotional health. Our pursuit of knowledge and dedication to self-improvement are vital for personal growth, leading to a more fulfilling and purposeful life. Investing in continuous learning and personal development—whether through reading, taking courses, or engaging in challenging and inspiring activities—can profoundly transform our lives and help stop overthinking. This journey isn't merely about acquiring new skills or knowledge; it's about fostering a resilient, adaptable mindset that supports emotional well-being and mental clarity.

When we commit to personal development, we are essentially nurturing our minds and emotions. Engaging in lifelong learning helps us stay mentally agile, reducing the risk of cognitive decline. It keeps our brains engaged and curious, which is crucial for mental health. Moreover, the process of setting and achieving personal goals boosts our self-esteem and confidence, providing a sense of accomplishment and purpose that combats feelings of anxiety and depression. Continuous learning also equips us with the tools to navigate life's challenges more effectively, fostering emotional resilience.

Something To Try: Continual Learning

- **Reading:** Enjoy books, articles, and journals to gain new perspectives and broaden your understanding. Set reading goals, establish a daily routine, and consider joining a book club. A reading journal enhances comprehension and retention.

- **Formal Education:** Enroll in courses and workshops to boost your skills and knowledge. Online courses, seminars, or further education keep you current, open new career opportunities, and expand your network. Certificates and degrees demonstrate commitment to growth and provide a sense of accomplishment.

- **Engaging Activities:** Step out of your comfort zone with challenging and inspiring activities. Travel, pursue hobbies, and volunteer to discover new passions and strengths. These experiences enrich your life and prevent fixation on work-related thoughts.

- **Structured Plan:** Set clear goals, gather resources, and create a timeline for your personal development journey. Consistency and time management are key. Review progress regularly, adjust plans, and celebrate achievements.

Personal development through continuous learning is a lifelong journey that leads to a fulfilling and balanced life. By dedicating yourself to growth, you can unlock your true potential and stop overthinking, ensuring your personal and professional aspirations align harmoniously.

———————◦○◦———————

Gratitude Practice

Getting caught up in the whirlwind of daily challenges and stressors is easy. Amidst this chaos, practicing gratitude can be a powerful way to shift perspective and enhance overall happiness. This section explores how keeping a gratitude journal or taking time each day to reflect on things to be grateful for can transform your outlook on life.

Gratitude is more than just a fleeting feeling; it's a profound appreciation for what has been received. Research shows that practicing gratitude brings numerous psychological, physical, and social benefits. It activates regions of the brain associated with dopamine, the "feel-good" hormone, and increases neural sensitivity to these areas, enhancing mood. Regularly expressing gratitude can reduce stress, improve sleep, and even boost the immune system.

Something To Try: Start a Gratitude Journal

One of the most effective ways to cultivate gratitude is by keeping a gratitude journal. This simple practice involves setting aside a few minutes daily to write down things you are thankful for. Here are some tips to get started:

1. **Choose a Journal:** Select a journal that you enjoy writing in. It could be a beautifully bound notebook or a simple, practical one. The key is to find something that resonates with you and encourages you to write regularly.

2. **Set a Routine:** Decide on a specific time of day to write in your journal. Many people find it helpful to do this in the morning to set a positive tone for the day, or in the evening to reflect on the day's events before going to bed.

3. **Be Specific:** Instead of writing general statements like "I'm grateful for my family," try to be specific. For example, "I'm grateful for the heartfelt conversation I had with my sister today" or "I'm grateful for the delicious homemade meal we shared as a family." Specificity helps to deepen your sense of gratitude.

4. **Reflect on Challenges:** Gratitude is about acknowledging the good times and the lessons learned during difficult times. Reflect on challenges and find something positive in them, such as personal growth or increased resilience.

5. **Consistency is Key:** Like any habit, consistency is crucial. Aim to write in your gratitude journal daily, even if it's just a few sentences. Over time, this practice will become a natural and integral part of your routine.

Daily Reflection Practice

In addition to—or instead of—journaling, you can incorporate daily gratitude reflections into your routine. This practice can be done anywhere and anytime, making it highly flexible and accessible.

Here are some ways to integrate gratitude reflections into your day:

- **Morning Gratitude Meditation:** Begin your day with a few minutes of gratitude meditation. Sit quietly, close your eyes, and consider three things you are grateful for. Visualize these things clearly in your mind and feel the appreciation in your heart.

- **Gratitude Walks:** Take a walk and use this time to reflect on the things you are grateful for. Being in nature can enhance this experience, allowing you to appreciate the beauty around you and feel a deeper connection to the world.

- **Gratitude Jar:** Place a jar in a visible spot in your home. Daily, write down something you are grateful for on a small piece of paper and put it in the jar. Over time, you'll have a jar full of positive moments to reflect on, especially when you need a boost.

- **Sharing Gratitude:** Make it a habit to share your gratitude with others. Whether it's expressing thanks to a colleague for their help or telling a friend how much you appreciate them, sharing gratitude can strengthen your relationships and spread positivity.

Incorporating gratitude practices into your daily routine can lead to profound changes in your life. By focusing on what you have rather than your lack, you cultivate a mindset of abundance and positivity. This shift in perspective can reduce feelings of envy, increase empathy, and improve overall well-being.

Gratitude also has a ripple effect. When you express gratitude, you inspire others to do the same. This creates a positive cycle, fostering a supportive and appreciative community around you.

Gratitude is a powerful practice that can significantly enhance your happiness and outlook on life. Whether through keeping a gratitude journal, daily reflections, or sharing your appreciation with others, making gratitude a regular part of your routine can lead to a more fulfilling and joyful life. Start today and watch as the simple act of being thankful transforms your world, one day at a time.

Self-Care

All the topics discussed in this chapter fall under the umbrella of self-care. Self-care means taking action to preserve or improve your health. It's essential to understand that self-care isn't selfish; in fact, it's selfish not to practice it. You're better equipped to support and care for others by prioritizing your well-being. Scientific studies have shown that regular self-care can reduce stress, improve mental health, and increase overall life satisfaction.

Self-care isn't just about indulgent spa days or splurging at the store. It's about getting the sleep you need to feel great and rejuvenated. It involves sharing a meal with people you love, fostering meaningful connections, and providing emotional support. Self-care encompasses various activities that contribute to your overall health and well-being, both physically and emotionally.

Bringing It All Together

To make self-care a consistent process, consider these tips:

- Schedule regular downtime in your calendar and treat it as non-negotiable.

- Establish a bedtime routine to ensure you get adequate, restful sleep.

- Engage in physical activity you enjoy, such as walking, jogging, yoga, or a workout.

- Nourish your body with healthy, balanced meals and hydrate adequately.

- Set aside time for hobbies and activities that bring you joy and relaxation.

- Practice mindfulness or meditation to center yourself and reduce stress.

- Connect with loved ones regularly to maintain strong, supportive relationships.

Boundaries are a crucial aspect of self-care. Only you can protect these times and make self-care a priority. Setting clear boundaries ensures you have the necessary space and time for self-care without external interruptions. By honoring these boundaries, you reinforce the importance of self-care and create a balanced, fulfilling life.

The healthier, more balanced, and empowered you are at your core, the more powerful and impactful you will be as a leader. Caring for yourself enhances your ability to lead with clarity, compassion, and resilience. Self-care is the foundation that allows you to thrive personally and professionally, enabling you to impact those around you positively.

As we wrap up this chapter, it's time to think bigger about how mindfulness can transform your leadership journey. Mindfulness isn't just about finding moments of calm—it's about cultivating a state of awareness and presence that permeates every aspect of your day. It's about integrating balance, focus, and creativity into your leadership style, making each moment more meaningful and impactful.

The following list offers a wealth of ideas to inspire you. From mindful breathing and gratitude journaling to creative visualization and mindful team interactions, these practices are designed to enhance your well-being and effectiveness. They encourage variety, diversity, and even a touch of playfulness in your approach to mindfulness.

Remember, mindfulness isn't a chore; it's the enriching pause between your responsibilities. It's what you do to center yourself, to connect with your inner wisdom, and to lead with greater clarity and compassion.

Here's to embracing mindfulness as a cornerstone of your leadership journey. May these ideas inspire you to cultivate a more mindful, balanced, and fulfilling workday.

50 Mindfulness Practices for Leaders: Enhancing Focus, Reducing Stress, and Improving Well-Being

1. **Mindful Coffee Breaks**: Savor your coffee, focusing on the taste and aroma.

2. **Mindful Appreciation of Colleagues**: Take a moment to appreciate and acknowledge your colleagues' efforts.

3. **Mindful Breathing Before Calls**: Take a few deep breaths before making or answering calls.

4. **Mindful Feedback**: Provide feedback mindfully, focusing on being constructive and supportive.

5. **Mindful Check-Ins**: Start meetings with a quick mindful check-in with your team.

6. **Mindful Gratitude Emails**: Send a quick email to thank someone for their help or support.

7. **Mindful Document Review**: Review documents with full attention to detail.

8. **Mindful Scheduling**: Schedule your day with mindfulness, avoiding overloading.

9. **Mindful Desktop Backgrounds**: Use calming images as your desktop background.

10. **Mindful Desktop Notifications**: Turn off unnecessary notifications to minimize distractions.

11. **Mindful Silence**: Schedule moments of complete silence throughout the day.

12. **Mindful Desk Objects**: Keep a small object on your desk to focus on during stressful moments.

13. **Mindful Problem Solving**: Approach problems with a calm and open mind.

14. **Mindful Creativity**: Spend time on creative tasks with full attention and curiosity.

15. **Mindful Use of Break Time**: Use break time to practice mindfulness instead of rushing through it.

16. **Mindful Task Initiation**: Start tasks with a mindful intention.

17. **Mindful Use of Office Supplies**: Handle office supplies like pens and paper with mindfulness.

18. **Mindful Personal Boundaries**: Set personal boundaries to maintain a work-life balance.

19. **Mindful Commute Preparation**: Prepare for your commute mindfully, whether working from home or traveling to the office.

20. **Mindful End-of-Week Reflection**: Reflect on the week mindfully every Friday.

21. **Mindful Appreciation of Small Wins**: Celebrate small achievements mindfully.

22. **Mindful Environment**: Arrange your office environment to promote calm and focus.

23. **Mindful Peer Support**: Offer support to colleagues mindfully.

24. **Mindful Task Delegation**: Delegate tasks with mindfulness and trust.

25. **Mindful Use of Technology**: Use technology tools mindfully to avoid distractions.

26. **Mindful Morning Routine**: Start your workday with a mindful morning routine.

27. **Mindful Presence in Meetings**: Be fully present in meetings, avoiding multitasking.

28. **Mindful Meeting Preparation**: Prepare for meetings with a calm and focused mind.

29. **Mindful Note Review**: Review your notes mindfully, focusing on the key points.

30. **Mindful Task Review**: Regularly review your task list mindfully.

31. **Mindful Use of Silence in Meetings**: Use moments of silence in meetings to encourage reflection.

32. **Mindful Desk Cleaning**: Clean your desk mindfully, appreciating the process.

33. **Mindful Filing**: Organize your files with mindfulness and attention to detail.

34. **Mindful Time Blocking**: Block out time in your calendar mindfully.

35. **Mindful Email Organization**: Organize your emails mindfully.

36. **Mindful Social Media Use**: Use social media mindfully, avoiding unnecessary scrolling.

37. **Mindful Inbox Checking**: Check your inbox mindfully, avoiding distractions.

38. **Mindful Lunch Breaks**: Take your lunch break mindfully, focusing on your food and surroundings.

39. **Mindful Use of Colors**: Use calming colors in your workspace to promote mindfulness.

40. **Mindful End-of-Day Closure**: Close your workday mindfully, reflecting on what went well.

41. **Mindful Participation in Webinars**: Engage in webinars and online training mindfully.

42. **Mindful Document Creation**: Create documents mindfully, focusing on clarity and purpose.

43. **Mindful Sharing of Knowledge**: Share your knowledge with colleagues mindfully.

44. **Mindful Conflict Resolution**: Approach conflicts with a mindful and open attitude.

45. **Mindful Adaptation to Change**: Adapt to changes in your work environment mindfully.

46. **Mindful Learning**: Engage in learning activities with full attention.

47. **Mindful Goal Review**: Regularly review your goals mindfully.

48. **Mindful Team Building**: Participate in team-building activities mindfully.

49. **Mindful Use of Break Rooms**: Use break rooms mindfully, focusing on relaxation and recharge.

50. **Mindful Desk Decorations**: Decorate your desk with items that promote mindfulness and calm.

Incorporating these mindfulness practices into your workday can enhance focus, reduce stress, and improve overall well-being for you and your team.

10

Leader's Toolkit

*"Give me six hours to chop down a tree and I will spend
the first four sharpening the axe." – Abraham Lincoln*

A Leader's Toolkit is a carefully curated set of tools, techniques, and resources designed to support leaders in their daily challenges. Much like a carpenter relies on a well-stocked toolbox to build and repair, leaders can turn to their toolkits for guidance, structure, and support in decision-making, stress management, and self-awareness. This toolkit isn't a one-size-fits-all solution but a versatile collection tailored to individual needs and situations.

The complexities of leadership often come with heightened responsibilities and pressures. Without effective strategies to manage these demands, leaders can succumb to overthinking, which can stymie productivity and harm well-being. A well-equipped toolkit provides immediate access to strategies and resources that promote efficient decision-making, foster mental clarity, and reduce unnecessary stress. It serves as both a preventive measure and a remedy, helping maintain composure and effectiveness when facing challenges.

Overthinking thrives in ambiguity and uncertainty. The Leader's Toolkit minimizes these factors by offering structured frameworks for decision-making, practices to stay present, and reflection exercises to gain insight. By providing clear, actionable steps and reducing the cognitive load associated with complex problems, the toolkit helps avoid the paralysis that often accompanies overthinking. It encourages a balanced approach to leadership—one that blends careful consideration with decisive action.

Empowerment comes from having the right tools at the right time. The Leader's Toolkit empowers leaders by equipping them with the resources needed to address specific overthinking tendencies. Each toolkit element is designed to enhance the ability to perform effectively. This sense of preparedness and capability fosters a proactive mindset, enabling leaders to tackle their roles with greater assurance and resilience.

The following sections provide detailed descriptions of each tool. By embracing and utilizing these strategies, leaders take a significant step toward becoming more confident, decisive, and empowered.

Agile Mindset

"Be like water making its way through cracks. Do not be assertive, but adjust to the object, and you shall find a way around or through it." – Bruce Lee

In the past decade, one of the biggest leadership changes has been the rise of agile approaches to delivering products, goods, and services. Embracing an agile mindset means thinking and working in a way that emphasizes flexibility, collaboration, and the ability to respond swiftly to change. This mindset comes from the principles of Agile, a methodology initially created for software development but now used widely across different industries. Agile values individuals and interactions over processes and tools, decision trees over comprehensive documentation, customer collaboration over contract negotiation, and responding to change over sticking to a fixed plan.

In today's rapidly changing business environment, adapting quickly is crucial. Traditional large-scale planning can be slow and inflexible, often leading to outdated strategies when they are implemented. In contrast, Agile allows for pivoting and adjusting approaches based on real-time feedback and changing conditions.

Constant communication and collaboration among team members and stakeholders is essential to keep up with the agile pace. Frequent interaction ensures that everyone is aligned and can share their insights, leading to more innovative solutions and a stronger sense of ownership among team members.

Breaking work into smaller, manageable chunks (sprints) allows for focus on specific tasks and deliverables, reducing the risk of burnout and boosting productivity. This approach also promptly identifies and addresses issues, preventing costly delays and rework.

Adopting an Agile Mindset as a Leader

Adopting an agile mindset requires a shift in perspective and behavior. It involves embracing flexibility, fostering collaboration, prioritizing continuous improvement, focusing on delivering value, empowering teams, and cultivating a growth mindset.

Embrace Flexibility: Leaders with an agile mindset understand that change is inevitable and embrace it rather than resist it. They are open to new ideas, willing to pivot when necessary, and comfortable with uncertainty. This flexibility allows them to effectively guide their teams through change and capitalize on new opportunities.

Foster a Collaborative Culture: Creating an environment where collaboration thrives is essential for agile success. Leaders encourage open communication, promote cross-functional teamwork, and ensure every team member feels valued and heard. This collaborative culture enhances innovation and problem-solving capabilities.

Prioritize Continuous Improvement: An agile mindset is rooted in the belief that there is always room for improvement. Leaders instill a continuous learning and development culture, encouraging their teams to seek feedback, experiment with new approaches, and learn from failures. This commitment to ongoing improvement drives progress and innovation.

Focus on Delivering Value: Agile leaders prioritize delivering value to customers and stakeholders. They ensure that every effort and resource is aligned with creating meaningful outcomes. Leaders can steer their teams towards achieving impactful results by keeping the end goal in mind and regularly assessing progress.

Empower and Trust Teams: Micromanagement is the antithesis of the agile mindset. Leaders empower their teams to take ownership of their work, make decisions, and solve problems independently. Trusting teams to deliver allows them to operate more efficiently and fosters a sense of accountability and pride in their work.

Cultivate a Growth Mindset: An agile leader embodies a growth mindset, believing that abilities and intelligence can be developed through dedication and hard work. This perspective encourages resilience, creativity, and a willingness to take on challenges. Leaders with a growth mindset inspire their teams to push beyond their comfort zones and continuously strive for excellence.

Managing Overthinking in an Agile Mindset

Overthinking can be a significant barrier to adopting an agile mindset, as it often leads to paralysis by analysis, stifles creativity, and hinders decision-making. However, an agile approach offers several strategies to mitigate overthinking and foster a more dynamic and productive environment. Here's how leaders can manage overthinking within the context of an agile mindset:

Embrace Incremental Progress: Agile delivers work in small, manageable increments. This approach helps break down complex projects into smaller tasks, reducing the tendency to overthink the entirety of a project. By concentrating on one piece at a time, leaders and teams can maintain focus and make steady progress without getting overwhelmed by the bigger picture.

Set Clear Priorities: In an agile framework, prioritizing tasks based on their value and impact is crucial. Establishing clear priorities helps leaders and teams concentrate on what matters most, thereby minimizing the tendency to overthink less critical details. Regularly revisiting and adjusting these priorities ensures everyone remains aligned and focused on delivering value.

Encourage Iterative Feedback: Regular feedback loops are a cornerstone of agile practices. By encouraging frequent check-ins and reviews, leaders can help teams quickly identify and address issues, preventing overthinking from escalating. This iterative approach allows for continuous improvement and adjustment, reducing the pressure to get everything perfect on the first try.

Promote a Fail-Fast Mentality: An agile mindset embraces experimentation and learning from failure. Leaders cultivate a culture where trying new ideas is encouraged, and failures are seen as valuable learning opportunities. This "fail-fast" mentality helps reduce the fear of making mistakes, which is a common trigger for overthinking. By normalizing failure as part of the process, leaders can help their teams take bold steps without being paralyzed by doubt.

Focus on Collaboration and Communication: Collaboration and open communication are vital in an agile environment. Leaders encourage team members to share their thoughts and concerns openly, which helps distribute the cognitive load and prevents individuals from overthinking in isolation. Collaborative problem-solving fosters a sense of shared responsibility and leverages diverse perspectives, leading to more effective and efficient solutions.

Implement Time-Boxing Techniques: Time-boxing is a technique used in Agile to limit the amount of time spent on specific tasks or activities. By setting fixed time frames for meetings, decision-making, and development sprints, leaders can prevent overthinking and ensure that progress continues steadily. This approach encourages focused effort and timely decision-making, reducing the tendency to dwell excessively on details.

Practice Mindfulness and Reflection: Incorporating mindfulness practices and regular reflection into the agile workflow can help manage overthinking. Leaders encourage their teams to take short breaks, practice mindfulness exercises, and reflect on their progress and challenges. These practices can help clear the mind, reduce stress, and foster a more balanced approach to work.

Use Data-Driven Decision-Making: Agile encourages the use of data and metrics to inform decisions. By relying on objective data rather than subjective speculation, leaders can reduce overthinking and make more confident, informed decisions. Tracking progress through key performance indicators (KPIs) and metrics helps maintain clarity and focus, ensuring that decisions are based on evidence rather than conjecture.

Continuous Learning and Improvement: An agile mindset values continuous learning and improvement. Creating an environment where learning from each iteration is prioritized, and insights are used to refine future work supports continual improvement and innovation. This approach helps leaders move forward with greater confidence and reduces the tendency to overthink by providing clear direction based on past experiences.

By embodying these principles, leaders can navigate the complexities of today's business environment, drive innovation, and achieve sustainable success. As they continue to face rapid changes and increasing competition, the agile mindset offers a powerful approach to stay ahead and thrive in the ever-evolving landscape.

Decision-Making Frameworks

"There is nothing so useless as doing efficiently that which should not be done at all." – Peter Drucker

Decision-making can often feel like navigating through a maze. Complex choices demand careful consideration, and the pressure to make the right call can lead to overthinking and paralysis.

However, structured decision-making frameworks can help us break down intricate decisions into manageable steps, ensuring clarity and reducing the mental load. This section explores several powerful tools, including decision matrices, flowcharts, and pros and cons lists, that can help us streamline our decision-making processes.

Decision Matrices: Evaluating Options with Precision

A decision matrix is a powerful tool that allows leaders to evaluate multiple options against a set of defined criteria. By quantifying the importance of each criterion and scoring each option accordingly, leaders can gain a clearer view of the best path forward.

Steps to Create a Decision Matrix:

1. **Identify Options and Criteria:** List all possible options and the important criteria for the decision.

2. **Assign Weights to Criteria:** Determine the importance of each criterion by assigning a weight (e.g., on a scale of 1 to 10).

3. **Score Each Option:** Evaluate each option against the criteria and assign a score (e.g., 1 to 5) for each criterion.

4. **Calculate Weighted Scores:** Multiply each score by the corresponding weight and sum the results for each option.

5. **Analyze Results:** The option with the highest total score is usually the most favorable choice.

Example:

Criteria	Weight	Option A	Option B	Option C
Cost	5	3	4	2
Time to Implement	3	4	3	5
Quality	4	5	3	4
Customer Impact	2	4	5	3
Total Score		43	38	37

In this example, Cost is most important, followed by Quality. Option A has the highest score and would be the preferred choice based on the weighted criteria because the combined factors outweigh a slightly higher cost. This insight may not surface without a decision matrix highlighting the bigger picture.

Decision matrices are invaluable for leaders striving to navigate complex choices with precision and clarity. By systematically breaking down options against a framework of weighted criteria, leaders can transcend subjective biases and make more informed, objective decisions. This structured approach enhances transparency and accountability and fosters a deeper understanding of the factors that drive successful outcomes.

When we embrace the use of decision matrices, we empower ourselves and our teams to move forward with confidence, ensuring that every decision is backed by thorough analysis and a clear rationale. Ultimately, consistently applying decision matrices can lead to more effective leadership, better strategic alignment, and a greater likelihood of achieving our organizational goals.

Eisenhower Matrix

The Eisenhower Matrix is a simple yet effective framework for prioritizing tasks. Named after Dwight D. Eisenhower, it helps individuals and leaders distinguish between what is truly important and what merely seems urgent.

Also known as the Urgent-Important Matrix, this tool traces its roots to Eisenhower's time management philosophy. Eisenhower, a five-star general in the United States Army, Supreme Commander of the Allied Forces during World War II, and the 34th President of the United States, had to make countless critical decisions. He famously said, "What is important is seldom urgent, and what is urgent is seldom important." This insight laid the foundation for the matrix that bears his name, helping people focus on what genuinely matters and avoid getting bogged down by immediate but insignificant tasks.

The Eisenhower Matrix is particularly beneficial for overcoming overwhelm. When burdened by a long to-do list, the matrix helps break down tasks into manageable categories, making it easier to discern what needs immediate attention and what can wait. This clarity is essential for enhancing productivity, enabling effective prioritization, and focusing on high-impact activities that drive progress and achieve goals more efficiently.

Additionally, the matrix improves decision-making by providing a clear framework for allocating time and resources wisely. It also plays a crucial role in balancing work and personal life, highlighting tasks that align with long-term goals and values and ensuring that professional responsibilities and personal well-being are maintained.

How to Use the Eisenhower Matrix

Step 1: **List Your Tasks:** List all the tasks you need to accomplish. This can include work-related duties, personal errands, and long-term projects. Be as comprehensive as possible.

Step 2: **Categorize Tasks:** Divide your tasks into four quadrants:

- **Quadrant I:** Urgent and Important (Do First) – Tasks in this quadrant require immediate attention and have significant consequences if not completed promptly. Examples include meeting deadlines, handling emergencies, and solving critical problems.

- **Quadrant II:** Important but Not Urgent (Schedule) – These tasks are crucial for achieving long-term goals but do not require immediate action. Examples include strategic planning, skill development, and building relationships. Schedule time to work on these tasks to prevent them from becoming urgent.

- **Quadrant III:** Urgent but Not Important (Delegate) – Tasks in this quadrant demand immediate attention but do not contribute significantly to long-term goals. Examples include routine emails, minor interruptions, and non-critical meetings. Delegate these tasks when possible.

- **Quadrant IV:** Not Urgent and Not Important (Don't Do) – These tasks are time-wasters and do not contribute to meaningful outcomes. Examples include unnecessary social media browsing, irrelevant meetings, and other distractions. Eliminate or minimize these activities.

Step 3: **Prioritize and Act:** Focus on Quadrant I tasks first, as they are both urgent and important. Next, allocate specific times in your schedule for Quadrant II tasks to ensure they receive the attention they deserve. Delegate Quadrant III tasks to others who can handle them, freeing up your time for more critical activities. Finally, aim to eliminate or reduce Quadrant IV tasks to optimize productivity.

Eisenhower Matrix Template

Do First	Schedule
Urgent & Important	Less Urgent but Important
I	II
Delegate	**Don't Do**
Urgent but less important	Neither Urgent nor Important
III	IV

Following a few practical tips is essential to make the most of the Eisenhower Matrix. Regularly review and update your matrix to reflect changing priorities and new tasks, ensuring it remains relevant and effective. Be realistic about the urgency and importance of each task to avoid overloading any one quadrant, which can lead to imbalance and inefficiency. Setting boundaries is crucial for protecting the time allocated for Quadrant II tasks and minimizing interruptions to focus on these important but not urgent activities. Lastly, periodically reflect on using the matrix, learning from your experiences, and adjusting your approach to find what works best for you.

The Eisenhower Matrix is a timeless tool that helps individuals and leaders prioritize tasks effectively, enhancing productivity and achieving a balanced life. By categorizing tasks based on urgency and importance, you can focus on what truly matters, make better decisions, and lead a more fulfilling life. Embrace this simple yet powerful framework and take control of your time, one quadrant at a time.

Flowcharts: Visualizing Process

Flowcharts are visual tools that outline the steps involved in any process, including the decision process. They help visualize the sequence of actions and the possible outcomes of each step. Being naturally visual beings, humans benefit greatly from seeing processes mapped out, as it enhances understanding and decision-making abilities. Flowcharts tap into this natural inclination, offering a clear and structured visualization of processes.

By outlining each step and its potential outcomes, flowcharts provide a streamlined overview that helps identify key actions and decisions quickly. This clarity and focus are invaluable for making swift, efficient choices and boosting confidence in the chosen course of action. Additionally, flowcharts help create organization and ensure that assumptions are tested without needing to research every potential outcome. For instance, a step can be included to validate whether taking action is better than doing nothing. Often, doing nothing is the right answer, but it gets overlooked. By incorporating this consideration into the flowchart, leaders can make quick, balanced, and well-informed decisions, leading to more effective leadership and successful outcomes.

Steps to Create a Decision Flowchart:

1. **Define the Decision Point:** Start with the main decision that needs to be made.

2. **List Possible Actions:** Identify the actions that can be taken at each step.

3. **Map Outcomes:** For each action, capture the possible results.

4. **Navigate to Best Outcome:** Looking at the flow of options and potential outcomes, follow the steps to the best solution.

Flowcharts can be as detailed or as simple as needed. They are powerful tools that can significantly enhance decision-making, providing clarity, structure, and insight. By visually mapping out each step, flowcharts help break down complex decisions into manageable parts, ensuring that no critical aspect is overlooked and that the focus remains on the right step at the right time.

Example Flowchart:

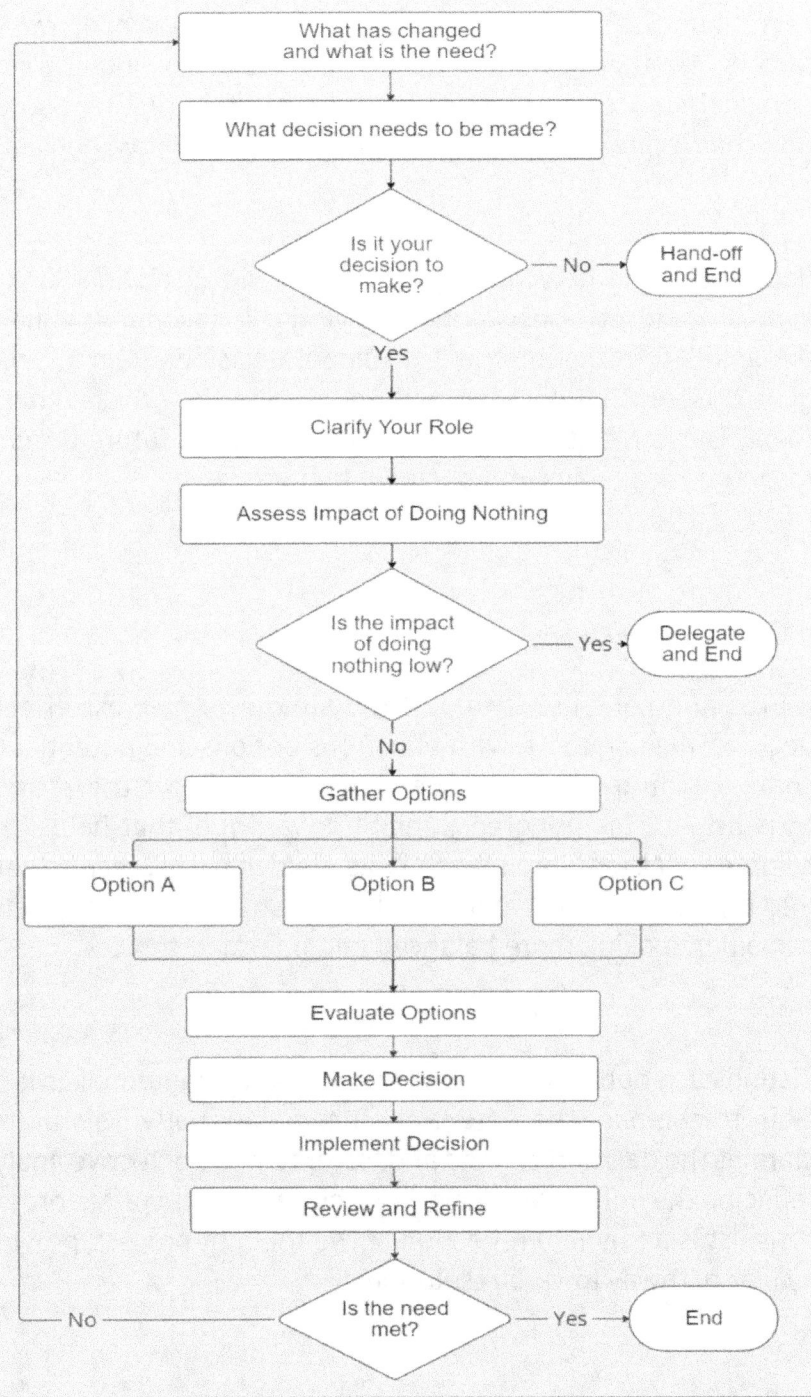

The decision flowchart template presented here is designed to guide through a systematic approach, asking the right questions at each stage and prompting thoughtful consideration of all relevant factors. Whether navigating strategic decisions, working through personal choices, or contributing to collective problem-solving, flowcharting can streamline the process and improve outcomes.

Routinely using flowcharting fosters a more disciplined and analytical mindset. Consistently applying this technique enhances the ability to make informed, confident decisions. Remember, the goal is to reach a decision and understand the process that led there. This understanding can be invaluable for future decisions, fostering continuous improvement and growth.

Pros and Cons Lists

A pros and cons list is one of the simplest yet most effective decision-making tools. With numerous options and potential outcomes, finding clarity can be challenging. Enter the pros and cons list—a time-honored, straightforward tool that helps distill complex decisions into manageable elements. This section delves into the power of pros and cons lists, illustrating how this method can aid in making more balanced and informed choices.

Listing each option's advantages and disadvantages makes it possible to compare the potential outcomes visually. This practice clarifies the decision at hand and fosters a more objective analysis, reducing the influence of emotional biases. A well-crafted pros and cons list is a tangible reflection of the thought process, providing a clear pathway toward resolution.

Steps to Create a Pros and Cons List:

1. **List the Options:** Write down the decision or options being considered.

2. **Identify:** List the pros and cons for each option.

3. **Evaluate the List:** Compare the pros and cons for each option.

Example:

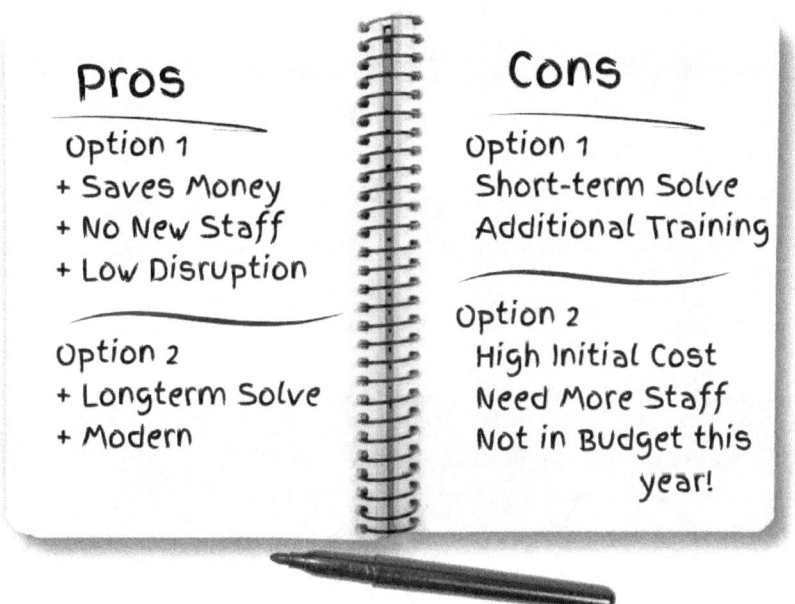

By breaking down the advantages and disadvantages of each option, a clear and comprehensive view of the potential outcomes can be gained. This method helps organize thoughts, uncover hidden factors, and encourage objectivity by presenting a balanced perspective.

The simplicity of a pros and cons list belies its effectiveness. It can be used for decisions big and small, providing clarity in moments of uncertainty and facilitating informed choices. By visualizing the potential benefits and drawbacks, options can be weighed more thoroughly, ensuring that all angles are considered.

Moreover, creating a pros and cons list can serve as a reflective exercise, helping to align decisions with values, goals, and the organization's broader vision. It fosters a disciplined approach to decision-making, minimizing the influence of emotional biases and promoting rational thinking.

Incorporating pros and cons lists into the decision-making toolkit empowers individuals to navigate complex situations more confidently and clearly. Honing this skill leads to well-reasoned decisions aligned with long-term objectives and the well-being of the team and organization.

Integrating Frameworks: A Holistic Approach

While each decision-making tool is powerful on its own, integrating these frameworks provides a comprehensive approach to complex decisions. For example, starting with a pros and cons list helps identify key criteria for a decision matrix. Then, a flowchart can map out the steps needed to implement the top choice from the decision matrix.

Structured decision-making frameworks equip leaders with the tools to navigate complex choices confidently. By breaking down decisions into manageable steps, overthinking is reduced, leading to informed, balanced decisions. Whether using a decision matrix to evaluate options, a flowchart to visualize the process, or a pros and cons list to weigh benefits and drawbacks, these tools provide clarity and structure, fostering effective leadership and positive outcomes.

Incorporating these frameworks into the decision-making toolkit transforms how challenges are approached, leading to more consistent and confident leadership. The key is to start with a clear understanding of objectives, apply the appropriate framework, and remain open to the insights each tool can provide.

Prioritization

"Out of clutter, find simplicity. From discord, find harmony. In the middle of difficulty lies opportunity." – Albert Einstein

The ability to prioritize effectively can be the difference between success and being overwhelmed. Prioritization is not just about managing time; it's about managing focus and energy. Leaders who master the art of prioritization can navigate complex challenges, make impactful decisions, and drive their teams toward strategic goals with clarity and confidence.

Prioritization is the practice of identifying what is most important and dedicating time and resources to those tasks. This approach allows leaders to enhance efficiency by focusing on high-priority tasks, which maximizes productivity and ensures critical tasks are completed efficiently. It also improves decision-making by clearly understanding what is most important, leading to more thoughtful and effective strategies. Additionally, prioritization reduces stress and overwhelm by managing the workload effectively and setting a positive example for the team. Most importantly, it ensures that daily tasks and projects align with the organization's overall strategic goals, driving progress and contributing to the broader mission.

The 80/20 Rule, also known as the Pareto Principle, is a powerful concept in prioritization. It states that roughly 80% of the results come from 20% of the efforts. This principle can be applied to various aspects of leadership and personal productivity. Leaders can achieve greater success with less effort by identifying the tasks, projects, or activities that yield the most significant results. It also helps in resource allocation by investing in the top 20% of initiatives that drive 80% of the results, optimizing resource utilization. Furthermore, the 80/20 Rule aids in time management, allowing leaders to dedicate their time to high-impact activities, enhancing productivity and effectiveness.

The 2-Minute Rule is another effective technique for managing small tasks. It states that if a task can be completed in two minutes or less, it should be done immediately. This rule helps avoid procrastination by encouraging immediate action on small tasks, reducing procrastination, and maintaining momentum. Completing small tasks quickly can create a sense of accomplishment, making it easier to tackle larger tasks. It also helps reduce clutter by handling minor tasks promptly, allowing leaders to focus on more significant priorities.

Integrating the 80/20 Rule and the 2-Minute Rule with the Eisenhower Matrix

The Eisenhower Matrix can be enhanced by incorporating the 80/20 Rule and the 2-Minute Rule:

- **80/20 Rule:** Identify the 20% of Quadrants I and II tasks that will yield 80% of the results. Focus your efforts on these high-impact tasks to maximize productivity.

- **2-Minute Rule:** Address tasks in Quadrants III and IV that can be completed in two minutes or less immediately to keep your to-do list manageable and prevent them from becoming distractions.

Mastering prioritization is a fundamental skill for effective and focused leadership. By leveraging the 80/20 and 2-Minute Rules, leaders can maximize their productivity, make better decisions, and reduce stress. This powerful combination ensures that leaders are not only doing things right but also doing the right things, driving their teams and organizations toward greater success.

Meeting Preparation

"You don't have to be the smartest person in the room, but if you're the most prepared, you'll be successful." - Magic Johnson

Meetings are a key part of professional life where decisions are made, collaboration occurs, and progress is driven. However, they can often be overwhelming and triggering for overthinking due to the pressure to contribute, fear of judgment, and the uncertainty of outcomes. Reflective, thoughtful, and focused preparation helps align with the meeting's purpose, contribute meaningfully, and address key concerns. This section will guide you through a structured approach to meeting preparation, highlighting the importance of clarity, intention, and active participation. Being well-prepared and knowing what to expect helps ease concerns, allowing for confident engagement.

This section provides a structured approach to meeting planning emphasizing the importance of clarity, intention, and active participation. By being well-prepared and knowing what to expect, you can ease concerns and engage confidently.

The Meeting Preparation Planner

Use the following planner to help you prepare for your meetings. This structured approach will help you cover all essential aspects, ensuring you are fully prepared and able to contribute effectively.

1. What is the purpose of this meeting?

Clearly define the primary goal of the meeting. Is it to make a decision, brainstorm ideas, update the team, or solve a problem?

2. What do I need from this meeting?

Identify your personal objectives. What information or decisions do you need to gain from the meeting to move forward with your tasks or responsibilities?

3. What can I contribute to this meeting?

Consider how you can add value. What insights, data, or suggestions can you bring to the table that will help achieve the meeting's goals?

4. What is my role in this meeting?

Understand your role, whether you are leading the meeting, facilitating discussion, presenting information, or participating in the dialogue. This clarity helps you prepare appropriately.

5. What is my intention for this meeting?

Set a clear intention for your participation. Are you there to listen and learn, to advocate for a particular outcome, or to support a colleague?

6. What questions do I need answered?

List any specific questions you need to ask to gather information, clarify doubts, or make informed decisions during the meeting.

7. What concerns me?

Identify any concerns or challenges you foresee related to the meeting topic. This will help you address them proactively.

8. What would make these concerns better?

Think about potential solutions or actions that could alleviate your concerns. This prepares you to discuss and address these issues constructively during the meeting.

The Meeting Preparation Planner offers a mindful, structured approach, guiding through essential questions and considerations to prepare for any meeting. Whether leading the discussion, presenting information, or participating in the dialogue, this template will help clarify objectives, contributions, and concerns, supporting confidence and mental clarity.

Effective meeting preparation isn't just a skill; it's a strategic advantage. This template helps you step into every meeting with confidence, clarity, and purpose.

Embracing "I don't know."

> "Real knowledge is to know the extent of one's ignorance." – Confucius

Nearly every leader faces the challenge of the fear of saying, "I don't know." This fear often triggers overthinking and over-preparing, leading to stress and inefficiency. It's essential to address this topic and overcome it.

In the professional world, having all the answers all the time is unrealistic. Confidently saying, "I don't know, but I can get that answer to you," demonstrates honesty, responsibility, and a commitment to finding solutions. Embracing uncertainty confidently, staying calm under pressure, and ensuring prompt follow-up are key skills.

Not always having an immediate answer can be daunting. However, acknowledging uncertainty is a sign of strength, not weakness. It shows honesty about limitations and dedication to providing accurate information. Embrace the power of "I don't know." Practice saying it out loud, yell it in the car, say it in the mirror, and let honesty guide you.

Admitting uncertainty builds trust, encourages collaboration, and demonstrates accountability. Honesty fosters trust among colleagues and clients.

How to Confidently Say "I Don't Know"

1. **Be Honest and Direct:** When faced with a question you can't answer, respond directly: "I don't know, but I can get that answer to you." Avoid making up information or giving vague responses to prevent misinformation and misunderstandings.

2. **Stay Calm and Composed:** Maintain a calm demeanor and breathe through it. Do not apologize unnecessarily. Keep your tone sincere and calm.

3. **Commit to Following Up:** Clearly state that you will find the necessary information and follow up promptly. For example: "I don't have that information at the moment, but I will look into it and get back to you by the end of the day."

4. **Set a Realistic Timeline:** Provide a reasonable timeframe for when you will have the answer. This sets expectations and demonstrates reliability. For example: "I'll need to check with the finance team. I should have an answer for you by tomorrow afternoon."

5. **Follow Up Promptly:** Make it a priority to gather the information and follow up within the promised timeframe. Even if you don't have a complete answer, update the person on your progress: "I'm still waiting on a response from the finance team, but I should have the information by tomorrow afternoon as expected."

By confidently saying, "I don't know, but I can get that answer to you," confidence and integrity are modeled to the team. Being honest, staying calm, and following up promptly show commitment to providing accurate information. Remember, no one expects to have all the answers. The willingness to find the right answers and dedication to supporting the team and clients matter immensely.

―――――◦―――――

Time Blocking

"The timing of your actions is important. Timing is everything." – Vikrmn

Time is one of the most precious resources. It's finite, non-renewable, and once spent, it can never be reclaimed. Managing time effectively can significantly impact productivity, well-being, and overall success. One strategy to protect and maximize this resource is time blocking. By scheduling time to align with energy levels and dedicating specific blocks for focused work, peak efficiency can be achieved while maintaining a healthy work-life balance.

Scheduling quality work time aligned with your energy levels involves dividing the day into blocks of time, each dedicated to a specific task or group of tasks. This method helps focus on one thing at a time, reducing distractions and the inefficiencies of multitasking. Essential tasks receive the attention they deserve by reserving time specifically for quality work.

Creating a daily template that reflects energy levels can be beneficial. For instance, if you're a morning person, block off the first few hours of the day for high-energy tasks and use the late afternoon for routine or administrative tasks when energy wanes. Treating time blocks as non-negotiable appointments and informing colleagues and family members of the schedule can help minimize interruptions.

By booking specific time slots for quality work, productivity is maximized, and important tasks are completed. Setting aside time to plan for the following week at the end of each week allows for identifying key tasks and allocating appropriate time blocks for each. Using a digital calendar or planner to map out time blocks visually, with color coding to identify different types of tasks quickly, can be very effective. Clearly defining the start and end of each time block and avoiding overrunning into the next block is crucial to maintaining the day's structure. Allowing for buffer times between tasks can account for overruns and unexpected interruptions, and overloading the schedule should be avoided to prevent stress and burnout.

Regularly reviewing time blocks to see what's working and what's not, adjusting the schedule as needed to better align with energy levels and changing priorities is crucial. Time blocking can be customized to fit anyone's schedule, regardless of personal or professional commitments. Identifying the most productive work hours and blocking them for deep work while using less productive times for meetings, emails, and administrative tasks helps balance time blocks for business development, client work, and administrative duties. It is also important to schedule time for self-care and personal development, allocate time blocks for studying, attending classes, and extracurricular activities, and ensure time for rest and recreation to avoid burnout.

Aligning Time Blocks with Your Energy Levels

1. **Identify Your Energy Peaks and Troughs:** Pay attention to when you feel most energetic and focused throughout the day. These are your peak times, and they should be reserved for your most critical and demanding tasks. Conversely, schedule less demanding tasks during your energy troughs.

2. **Categorize Your Tasks:** Group your tasks based on their nature and energy requirements. High-energy tasks might include creative work, strategic planning, or problem-solving. Low-energy tasks could be administrative work, email management, or routine check-ins.

3. **Create a Daily Template:** Create a daily template reflecting your energy levels. For instance, if you're a morning person, block off the first few hours of the day for high-energy tasks. Use the late afternoon for routine or administrative tasks when your energy wanes.

4. **Protect Your Time Blocks:** When you have a deep focus task or deliverable, treat your time blocks as non-negotiable appointments. Inform colleagues and family members of your schedule to minimize interruptions.

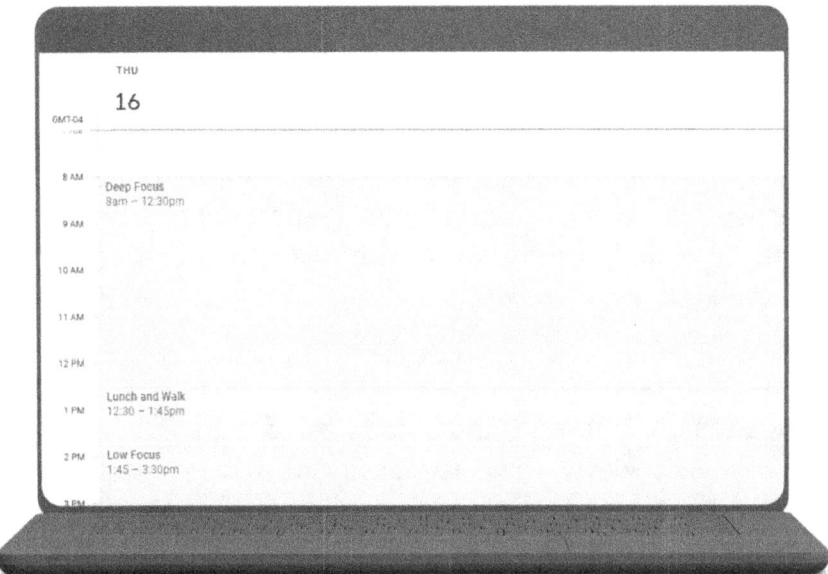

Time blocking is a powerful strategy for protecting time and aligning work with natural energy levels. By thoughtfully planning and consistently applying this technique, including booking specific time for quality work, productivity can be enhanced, a better work-life balance can be maintained, and goals can be achieved with greater ease and satisfaction. Embrace the power of time blocking to transform how time is managed.

Boundary Setting

"Love yourself enough to set boundaries. Your time and energy are precious. You get to choose how you use it." – *Anna Taylor*

One powerful strategy to combat overthinking is to establish and maintain clear boundaries. Boundaries are guidelines, rules, or limits that a person sets to define what are reasonable, appropriate, and expected ways for others to behave and how the leader will respond when someone crosses those limits. In a leadership context, boundaries help clarify roles, responsibilities, and expectations, providing a framework within which leaders and their teams can operate effectively.

Boundaries are often misunderstood as barriers that isolate us from others. However, they are not meant to be walls that keep people out but rather bridges that allow for healthy, respectful interactions. They are essential for creating a balanced and productive work environment, enabling leaders to focus on their core responsibilities without being overwhelmed by unnecessary tasks or undue stress.

Clear boundaries help delineate responsibilities, ensuring that everyone knows their roles and what is expected of them. This clarity reduces ambiguity and the tendency to overthink every decision. Leaders with well-defined responsibilities can focus on what truly matters rather than being distracted by tasks that fall outside their purview.

Leaders often feel compelled to oversee every aspect of their team's work, leading to micromanagement and overthinking. By setting boundaries, leaders can exercise the discipline to trust their team members and delegate effectively. This empowers the team and allows leaders to concentrate on strategic initiatives and high-level decisions.

Boundaries set the stage for a sustainable and healthy work environment. They prevent burnout by ensuring that leaders and their teams are not overburdened. With appropriate boundaries in place, leaders can maintain a work-life balance, make more informed decisions, and approach challenges with a clear, focused mind.

Tips for Keeping Healthy Boundaries

1. **Communicate Clearly and Consistently**: Effective boundaries start with clear communication. Effective leaders articulate their expectations, responsibilities, and limits to their team members. Regularly revisit these boundaries in team meetings and one-on-one discussions to ensure everyone remains aligned. Clear communication helps prevent misunderstandings and reduces the likelihood of overthinking due to ambiguity.

2. **Learn to Say No**: One of the most challenging aspects of maintaining boundaries is the ability to say no. Leaders often feel obliged to take on additional tasks or accommodate every request, leading to overload and overthinking. By learning to say no to tasks that fall outside their core responsibilities or that they do not have the capacity to handle, leaders can protect their time and energy for more critical issues. Saying no respectfully and assertively is a vital skill in maintaining healthy boundaries.

3. **Regularly Review and Adjust Boundaries**: Boundaries are not static; they need to be reviewed and adjusted as circumstances change. Effective leaders regularly assess their workload, responsibilities, and the effectiveness of their boundaries. Are there areas where they are still overreaching? Are there new responsibilities that require boundary adjustments? By staying attuned to their needs and the needs of their team, leaders can ensure that their

boundaries remain relevant and effective.

Boundaries are a fundamental aspect of effective leadership, particularly in managing overthinking. They provide clarity of responsibility, discipline to avoid overreach, and a foundation for success. Embrace boundaries not as limitations but as essential tools for empowering yourself and your team. In doing so, you pave the way for more decisive leadership, strategic alignment, and a thriving organizational culture.

Professional Network

"The richest people in the world look for and build networks; everyone else looks for work." — Robert Kiyosaki

In today's interconnected professional landscape, the value of a robust network cannot be overstated. A well-established professional network serves as a gateway to new opportunities, a critical support system, and a catalyst for personal and professional growth.

A professional network is an invaluable asset, composed of relationships with colleagues, mentors, industry experts, and other professionals who can provide insights, advice, opportunities, and support throughout your career. The true value of a professional network lies in its ability to open doors that might otherwise remain closed. Studies show that a significant percentage of professional hires—around 70-85%—are made through leveraging professional networks. This statistic underscores the adage that it's often who you know, not just what you know, that propels your career forward.

Beyond job opportunities, a diverse network offers a wealth of knowledge and experiences. Engaging with peers from different backgrounds and industries allows you to gain new perspectives, learn best practices, and stay abreast of the latest trends and developments. This continuous learning is crucial for career development and advancement. Mentors and industry leaders within your network can provide valuable career advice, guidance on skill development, and insights into potential career paths. Moreover, recommendations and endorsements from your network can significantly enhance your professional reputation.

A professional network also acts as a vital support system during challenging times. Whether facing a career transition, seeking advice on a difficult project, or needing encouragement, your network can provide the necessary support and resources. This support extends beyond professional boundaries, enriching your personal and professional life.

The benefits of cultivating a strong professional network are numerous and far-reaching. Increased visibility and credibility are among the most significant advantages. Being active in your professional community raises your profile and establishes you as a knowledgeable and credible professional. This can lead to speaking engagements, invitations to join panels, and other opportunities to showcase your expertise. Networking also fosters collaboration, enabling you to work with others who have complementary skills and knowledge. Such collaborations often lead to innovative solutions, creative projects, and successful ventures that you might not achieve alone.

A strong network provides career resilience by offering multiple job opportunities and professional growth avenues. In times of economic uncertainty or job loss, a solid network can be a lifeline, helping you navigate the job market and find new opportunities. Engaging with diverse professionals can boost your confidence, improve your communication skills, and broaden your horizons. These relationships can enrich your personal and professional life, providing a sense of belonging and support.

Building a professional network requires intentionality and effort. Attending industry events and conferences is a powerful way to meet professionals from your field and beyond. Leveraging social media platforms like LinkedIn allows you to connect with colleagues, join professional groups, and engage in discussions. Joining professional associations related to your field can provide access to networking events, resources, and a community of like-minded professionals. Seeking mentors and advisors who can provide guidance and support is also crucial for personal and professional growth. Volunteering for industry-related events, committees, or community service projects can help you build connections while giving back to your community.

Once you have built a network, it is essential to leverage it effectively. Staying engaged and connected with your contacts through regular communication is key. Offering your expertise, support, and assistance builds trust and reciprocity, making your network more willing to help you in return. It is crucial to be strategic and targeted in identifying key individuals who can help you achieve specific career goals. Follow up with thank-you notes or messages after any networking interaction to reinforce the relationship and leave a positive impression.

Maintaining a professional network requires ongoing effort and care. Regularly check in with your contacts to maintain the relationship, share updates, congratulate them on their achievements, and offer support when needed. Sharing valuable content, such as articles, blog posts, or industry insights, with your network positions you as a thought leader and keeps you on your contacts' radar. Authenticity is key to building and maintaining meaningful relationships. Be yourself, show genuine interest in others, and build connections based on mutual respect and trust. Ensure your contact information and professional profiles are current, making it easy for your network to reach you and stay connected.

A professional network is a powerful asset that can significantly impact your career trajectory and personal growth. You can unlock many opportunities and support by understanding its value, actively building and maintaining it, and leveraging it effectively. Remember, networking is not just about what others can do for you but also about how you can contribute to and support your professional community. Embrace the networking journey with an open mind and a genuine heart, and you will find that the connections you build will be among the most valuable resources in your professional life.

Evolving Your Toolkit

"Do the best you can until you know better. Then when you know better, do better." – Maya Angelou

As we wrap up this chapter on the Leader's Toolkit, it's essential to recognize that a toolkit isn't a static collection of resources. As individuals grow and circumstances change, so should the tools relied upon. This dynamic nature is what makes a toolkit truly effective—its ability to adapt and expand to meet the ever-changing demands of leadership.

The journey as a leader is marked by continuous learning and development. Encountering new challenges and gaining deeper insights into leadership styles leads to discovering new tools to enhance effectiveness. Stay open to exploring different strategies and approaches. Attend workshops, read widely, and engage with other leaders to learn about the tools and techniques they find valuable. The toolkit can continuously be refined and expanded by remaining curious and proactive.

When integrating new tools, consider how they align with personal leadership styles and the specific challenges faced. Experiment with different resources and observe their impact on decision-making processes, stress levels, and overall effectiveness. Don't be afraid to discard tools that don't work and replace them with ones that do. The goal is to build a personalized set of resources that truly supports unique needs and strengths.

Leadership often requires innovative thinking and a willingness to try new things. Embrace creativity when curating the toolkit. Think beyond traditional tools and consider unconventional resources that offer fresh perspectives or solutions. Creativity can lead to powerful and effective additions, whether a unique mindfulness practice, a novel decision-making framework, or an unexpected source of inspiration.

Ultimately, the toolkit's effectiveness lies in its personalization. What works for one leader may not work for another. Tailor the toolkit to fit individual preferences, strengths, and goals. Regularly review and update resources to ensure they remain relevant and effective. Personalization enhances the utility of the tools and empowers leaders to act with greater confidence and authenticity.

In summary, a leader's toolkit is a living, evolving collection of resources designed to support growth and effectiveness. By continuously seeking out and incorporating new tools, embracing creativity, and personalizing the approach, building a toolkit that minimizes overthinking and empowers clear and confident leadership is possible. Remember, the leadership journey is ever-changing, and so should the tools used to navigate it.

II

Team Empowerment Strategies

"Leadership is the capacity to translate vision into reality."
– Warren Bennis

E mpowering a team is one of a leader's most vital responsibilities. In today's dynamic and fast-paced business environment, inspiring and enabling a team to achieve its highest potential can make the difference between merely surviving and truly thriving. This chapter delves into the top strategies leaders can employ to empower their teams effectively.

By exploring the foundational principles of delegation, communication, trust-building, and continuous development, we uncover how to create an environment where team members feel valued, motivated, and equipped to contribute their best work. We also examine the importance of recognizing contributions, fostering an inclusive culture, and leading by example.

Empowerment goes beyond simple task assignments; it involves cultivating a sense of ownership, encouraging innovation, and facilitating personal and professional growth. Additionally, empowering a team minimizes overthinking for both leaders and team members. When empowered, team members gain confidence in their decision-making abilities and take ownership of their responsibilities. This autonomy reduces the need for constant supervision and close management, alleviating the mental burden on leaders. For team members, empowerment increases job satisfaction and a sense of control over their work, reducing anxiety and the tendency to second-guess their actions.

The science behind this is rooted in psychology and organizational behavior. Studies have shown that empowerment is linked to lower stress levels and higher job satisfaction. According to Self-Determination Theory (SDT), individuals have basic psychological needs for autonomy, competence, and relatedness. When these needs are met, individuals experience higher levels of intrinsic motivation and well-being. Empowering leadership practices satisfy these needs by providing autonomy, opportunities for skill development, and a supportive social environment.

Empowering teams also fosters a culture of trust and open communication, where mistakes are viewed as learning opportunities rather than failures. This mindset shift reduces the fear of making errors, a common source of overthinking. Leaders can focus more on creative solutions and proactive problem-solving rather than being paralyzed by the fear of making wrong decisions.

Welcome to a journey of empowering leadership, where a team's success becomes the cornerstone of a leader's own success. Through the principles and practices outlined in this chapter, leaders will learn how to build a thriving, resilient, and innovative team while fostering a work environment that minimizes overthinking and maximizes potential.

Vision

Effective leadership involves communicating a clear vision and setting achievable goals. This clarity ensures everyone understands the direction and their roles in achieving the desired outcomes. A well-articulated vision is a guiding star, providing purpose and motivation, while clearly defined goals offer a roadmap to success.

The term "vision" refers to a mental image of the future. It's called a vision because it encapsulates an ideal concrete state an organization aspires to achieve. This forward-looking perspective helps align efforts and inspires collective action toward common objectives. A vision transcends the present and paints a picture of a desirable future, creating a sense of purpose and direction.

Skipping the creation of a vision and jumping straight into writing goals is a common pitfall for many leaders, driven by the urgency to produce tangible results and the pressure to demonstrate progress. This tendency often stems from a misconception that immediate action and visible achievements are more valuable than the foundational work of envisioning the future. However, this approach can lead to a significant misalignment within the team, as goals without a clear vision may lack coherence and purpose.

Vision taps into our innate human tendency towards visual thinking, providing a meaningful connection that aligns and inspires those involved. Leaders who learn to articulate clear, concrete, and aspirational visions for near to mid-term goals harness the same energy that drives entire organizations forward, creating momentum and unity at all levels.

Humans are fundamentally visual beings. Our brains process images 60,000 times faster than text, and about 90% of the information transmitted to our brains is visual. This visual nature influences how we understand and engage with the world, making vision a critical component of effective leadership.

A compelling vision transforms abstract ideas into tangible realities people can see, feel, and believe in. It paints a picture of the future that is both inspiring and attainable, providing a clear direction that motivates action. When leaders articulate this vision, they tap into their teams' collective imagination, fostering a shared sense of purpose and commitment.

A well-crafted vision serves multiple purposes in leadership. It acts as a guiding star, providing direction and clarity amidst the complexities and uncertainties of daily operations. It inspires and motivates, creating a sense of excitement and anticipation about the future. It also aligns efforts, ensuring everyone meets the same goals and priorities.

For leaders, articulating a clear and compelling vision is a critical skill. It requires a deep understanding of the organization's values, goals, and potential and the ability to communicate these elements in a way that resonates with others. This involves defining what the future looks like and explaining why it matters and how it can be achieved.

While company vision statements are essential, the power of vision also extends to smaller initiatives. A clear and aspirational vision benefits each project, team goal, or strategic effort. These smaller visions provide the same benefits as a company-wide vision: direction, motivation, and alignment.

When crafting a vision for smaller initiatives, focus on the project's specific goals and outcomes. The vision should paint a picture of what success looks like and why it is important. Remember, a vision is concrete and specific yet aspirational enough to inspire and motivate.

Practice Vision Exercise

Based on what we have learned, let's look at three examples of visions for implementing a new learning experience. In this exercise, you will explore three distinct and powerful visions for your IT team to consider.

Vision 1: Empowering Continuous Learning

Create a dynamic, user-friendly learning platform that empowers employees to manage their professional growth. Integrate personalized learning paths to meet current and future skill needs, fostering a culture of continuous improvement and innovation.

Vision 2: Enhancing Engagement through Interactive Learning

Develop an engaging, interactive learning experience using gamification, social learning tools, and real-time feedback. Address immediate skill development while preparing the workforce for future challenges, fostering collaboration and a sense of community.

Vision 3: Building a Future-Ready Workforce

Imagine a day where employees receive real-time, personalized recommendations on their devices, helping them master new skills on the spot. Picture a culture where upskilling happens naturally throughout the workday, ensuring our team is always ahead of industry trends. This continuous learning environment empowers everyone to contribute to our success, driving individual growth and organizational excellence.

Which vision stands out as the best vision due to its vivid imagery and strong emotional impact? The best vision paints a clear picture of a future workplace where learning seamlessly integrates into daily activities, tailoring development to each employee's needs. By describing specific scenarios, such as employees receiving real-time, personalized recommendations on their devices and mastering new skills on the spot, this vision brings the abstract concept of continuous learning to life in a tangible and relatable way.

Emotionally, this vision emphasizes empowerment, making employees feel valued and supported in their professional growth. The depiction of a vibrant and innovative work culture evokes excitement about being part of an organization that stays ahead of industry trends. It also fosters a strong sense of community and collective success by highlighting that individual growth contributes to organizational excellence, promoting a shared purpose.

Moreover, this vision is forward-looking and relevant, focused on preparing the workforce for future challenges, which is essential for long-term success. The inclusion of real-time feedback suggests adaptability and a commitment to staying ahead in a rapidly changing industry. Its inclusive approach addresses the needs of all employees, ensuring that everyone can upskill naturally throughout their workday, thus speaking to a wide audience within the organization.

In summary, Vision 3 is the best because it creates a compelling, clear, and emotionally resonant picture of the future. Combining practical elements with motivational language fosters a sense of excitement and empowerment that can inspire employees and align their efforts toward achieving this shared goal.

Practical Steps for Crafting Vision

1. **Understand the Purpose**: Start by understanding the initiative's core purpose. What are you trying to achieve, and why does it matter? This clarity of purpose forms the foundation of your vision.

2. **Define Success**: Paint a clear picture of what success looks like. Be specific and concrete but also aspirational. What will the future look like when you achieve your goals?

3. **Communicate Clearly**: Articulate your vision in a way that is clear, compelling, and easy to understand. Use vivid, visual language that helps people see and feel the future you are describing.

4. **Inspire and Motivate**: Ensure that your vision taps into your team's deeper motivations and aspirations. Help them see how their work contributes to a larger purpose and why it matters.

5. **Align Efforts**: Use your vision to align efforts and priorities. Ensure that everyone understands how their work fits into the bigger picture and how they can contribute to achieving the vision.

6. **Reinforce Consistently**: Consistently reinforce your vision through your actions, communications, and decisions. Show your commitment to the vision and inspire others to do the same.

The power of vision is undeniable. Whether crafting a company-wide vision statement or a vision for a smaller initiative, the ability to articulate a clear, concrete, and aspirational picture of the future is a critical skill for leaders. By tapping into our innate visual nature, leaders can align and inspire their teams, creating a shared sense of purpose and direction that drives success at all levels. As a leader, learning to craft and communicate vision is not just about setting goals; it's about creating a compelling story that everyone can believe in and work towards, turning abstract ideas into tangible realities.

SMARTER Goals

Considering the pace of business, the traditional approach to setting annual goals can feel increasingly irrelevant. The business landscape is ever-evolving, driven by rapid technological advancements, shifting market demands, and unexpected global events. Leaders must embrace a more agile and dynamic goal-setting approach, ensuring their objectives remain meaningful and relevant.

Annual goals often stem from a rigid, linear planning model that assumes a predictable and stable environment. This method can lead to several pitfalls, including inflexibility, as the static nature of annual goals hinders responsiveness to new opportunities or threats. Additionally, goals set at the beginning of the year may become irrelevant as conditions change, resulting in a lack of alignment with current priorities. This irrelevance can demotivate teams, especially when they see more urgent and relevant tasks emerging, leading to decreased engagement and productivity.

Comparing Agile Goal Setting to Annual Goal Setting

Aspect	Annual Goal Setting	Agile Goal Setting
Time Frame	Yearly	Quarterly or Monthly
Flexibility	Rigid, difficult to adjust	Highly adaptable, allows for regular changes
Feedback Frequency	Infrequent, often annual	Frequent, often weekly or bi-weekly
Relevance	Can become obsolete as context changes	Maintains relevance through continuous review
Adaptability	Limited, slow to respond to change	High, quickly adjusts to new information
Motivation	Can wane over time	Sustained through regular milestones
Learning Opportunities	Limited to end-of-year reviews	Continuous, through regular check-ins

Evolving Goals in Real-Time

Leaders must shift from a static to a dynamic goal-setting approach to lead effectively in a fast-changing environment. One way to achieve this is by embracing shorter time frames. Breaking down annual goals into shorter, more manageable periods, such as quarterly or monthly, allows for regular reassessment and adjustment based on current realities. By regularly reviewing and recalibrating goals, leaders can ensure that objectives remain aligned with the evolving landscape, keeping them relevant and teams engaged.

Fostering continuous feedback is another crucial strategy. Creating a culture where team members can voice observations and suggestions ensures that goals are adjusted in real time to reflect the latest insights and conditions. Open communication channels are essential for gathering input from all levels of the organization. Leaders must listen actively and be willing to pivot based on this feedback, thereby enhancing the responsiveness and effectiveness of goal-setting processes.

Aligning goals with the organization's vision and values is also vital. Regardless of how frequently goals are updated, they must remain aligned with the organization's overarching vision and values. This alignment provides a stable foundation amid change, giving teams a clear sense of purpose and direction. Reinforcing the connection between short-term goals and the long-term vision helps maintain coherence and motivation, even as specific objectives evolve.

Lastly, prioritizing adaptability is essential for thriving in a dynamic environment. Encouraging a mindset of adaptability among teams helps them view changes not as disruptions but as opportunities for growth and innovation. Leaders should demonstrate flexibility and resilience by example, showing that adaptability is a strength and a critical component of success in an agile world. By leading with this mindset, leaders can foster a culture that is better equipped to navigate and capitalize on the inevitable changes and challenges that arise.

Making Goals Meaningful and Relevant

1. **Set SMARTER Goals:** Traditional SMART goals (Specific, Measurable, Achievable, Relevant, Time-bound) are a good starting point, but in a fast-changing environment, adding the elements of **Evaluation** and **Re-adjustment** makes them SMARTER. Regularly evaluate progress and be willing to re-adjust goals to ensure they remain aligned with current priorities and realities.

2. **Focus on Outcomes, Not Tasks:** Shift the focus from task-based to outcome-based goals. This approach encourages innovation

and flexibility in achieving objectives. Clearly define the desired outcomes and empower teams to determine the best paths to achieve them. This fosters ownership and creativity.

3. **Integrate Learning and Development:** Incorporate goals that promote continuous learning and development. This ensures that teams always grow and adapt their skills to meet new challenges. Encourage a culture of curiosity and lifelong learning. Make professional development an integral part of goal setting.

To support the transition from traditional annual goal setting to a more agile approach, here is some key guidance to set leaders up for success. First, embrace shorter time frames by breaking down annual goals into quarterly or monthly objectives, allowing for regular reassessment and alignment with current realities.

Next, foster a culture of continuous feedback, encouraging team members to voice their observations and suggestions. This will ensure that goals are adjusted in real-time based on the latest insights. Align all goals with the organization's overarching vision and values, providing a stable foundation and a clear sense of purpose amid change.

Prioritize adaptability by encouraging a mindset that views changes as opportunities for growth and innovation, demonstrating flexibility and resilience as a leader. By following this guidance, leaders can effectively transition to agile goal setting, keeping objectives relevant, maintaining team engagement, and enhancing the organization's ability to respond to a rapidly changing environment.

In a world where change is the only constant, leaders must move beyond the outdated practice of annual goal-setting. By adopting a more agile and dynamic approach, goals can remain meaningful and relevant, driving strategic alignment and empowering teams to thrive. Embrace the journey of continual reassessment and adaptation, and you'll find that your organization is not only surviving but flourishing in the face of change.

The Power of Words

As leaders, the words chosen aren't just about conveying information; they shape perceptions, influence behaviors, and drive organizational culture. Word choice in leadership goes beyond simple communication—it's about inspiration, motivation, and influence. This section explores the critical aspects of word choice, the balance between inspiration and authenticity, and how neuro-linguistic programming (NLP) can enhance leadership effectiveness.

Leaders have the unique responsibility of guiding teams toward a shared vision. The words used to articulate this vision can inspire, motivate, and energize. Inspirational language fosters a sense of purpose and belonging, encouraging everyone to commit fully to their roles and collective goals.

Think about the difference between saying, "There is a lot of work to do," and "There is a tremendous opportunity to achieve something great together." The latter acknowledges and frames the challenge as a positive, shared endeavor. This subtle shift in wording can significantly impact team morale and motivation.

While inspiration is vital, it is important to avoid the trap of forced positivity. Authenticity is a cornerstone of effective leadership. Consistently painting an overly rosy picture risks losing credibility and trust. Team members are perceptive and can often see through insincere attempts to sugarcoat reality.

The key is to balance optimism with realism. Acknowledge challenges honestly while framing them as surmountable obstacles. For instance, instead of saying, "Everything is perfect," say, "We are facing some significant challenges, but I am confident in our ability to overcome them with our collective strengths."

Negative language can negatively affect team dynamics and individual performance. Phrases that focus on problems without offering solutions can create a culture of fear and discouragement. Leaders are at their best when mindful of how they address issues, ensuring their language is solution-oriented and empowering.

For example, instead of saying, "This project is failing," say, "We need to identify where we are falling short and develop strategies to improve." This approach acknowledges the problem while also focusing on proactive solutions.

Leveraging NLP in Leadership

Neuro-linguistic programming (NLP) is a psychological approach that explores the relationships between how we think (neuro), how we communicate (linguistic), and our behavioral patterns (programming). NLP offers a range of techniques that leaders can use to enhance their communication, build rapport, and influence more effectively.

Using NLP to Enhance Communication

- **Reframing:** Reframing involves changing how a situation or statement is perceived by altering its context or meaning. Leaders can use reframing to shift perspectives and encourage a more positive outlook. For example, instead of viewing a setback as a failure, it can be reframed as a learning opportunity that brings the team closer to success.

- **Anchoring:** Anchoring is a technique used to evoke a specific emotional state by associating it with a particular stimulus. Leaders can use anchoring to help their team access positive emotions such as confidence and motivation. For instance, starting meetings with a success story or a moment of celebration can anchor the team in a positive and productive state.

Language Patterns in NLP

1. **Positive Presuppositions:** Language that presupposes positive outcomes can subtly influence the team's mindset. For example, saying, "When we achieve our goals," instead of "If we achieve our goals," presupposes success and fosters a sense of certainty and confidence.

2. **Embedded Commands:** Embedded commands are subtle suggestions embedded within a larger sentence. For example, a leader might say, "As you consider the new project, you might find yourself getting excited about the possibilities." The embedded command "getting excited about the possibilities" encourages a specific emotional response without being overtly directive.

3. **Metaphors and Stories:** Metaphors and stories are powerful tools in NLP for conveying complex ideas and inspiring action. Leaders can use stories to illustrate key points, share experiences, and create a shared vision. A well-told story can resonate deeply and leave a lasting impact on the team. For example, when the team is in the middle of a complex problem, a leader might use the metaphor of a jigsaw puzzle and say, "It's true we may not be able to fit all the pieces together yet, so let's look for the corners and edge pieces to frame this puzzle."

The words chosen by leaders are more than just communication tools; they're instruments of influence and inspiration. Balancing authentic optimism with realism fosters a positive and productive organizational culture. Incorporating NLP techniques into leadership communication can further enhance the ability to connect, inspire, and motivate teams.

On the leadership journey, every word chosen can shape the team's reality. Embrace this responsibility with mindfulness and intentionality, knowing that words can inspire greatness and drive meaningful change.

Emotional Intelligence

Emotional intelligence (EI) is the ability to understand, manage, and effectively express one's own feelings and to understand and influence the emotions of others. This concept, first popularized by psychologist Daniel Goleman, encompasses five key components: self-awareness, self-regulation, motivation, empathy, and social skills. Leaders with high EI can navigate the complexities of human emotions, creating positive interactions and fostering a collaborative environment. However, it's equally crucial to cultivate EI within the entire team to enhance overall performance and well-being.

Emotional intelligence is crucial for leaders, team dynamics, and organizational success. Leaders with high EI can communicate more effectively, listening actively and clearly conveying their thoughts and ideas, which fosters better understanding and co-operation among team members. When leaders and team members possess high EI, it enhances overall communication, reduces conflicts, and creates a harmonious work environment.

EI allows leaders and teams to handle conflicts gracefully, understand different perspectives, and find mutually beneficial solutions. By demonstrating empathy and understanding, emotionally intelligent leaders build stronger relationships with their team members, enhancing trust and loyalty. Likewise, team members with high EI contribute to a supportive and collaborative culture.

The emphasis on emotional intelligence is increasing in the modern workplace for several reasons. First, managing emotions and relationships becomes critical to achieving success as work becomes more complex and interconnected. A diverse workforce brings varied perspectives and emotional dynamics, and teams need emotional intelligence to navigate and leverage this diversity effectively. Additionally, the rise of remote work requires leaders and team members to connect and engage virtually, making EI essential for maintaining team cohesion and morale.

Moreover, with greater awareness of mental health issues, leaders and teams need to be attuned to each other's emotional well-being and provide appropriate support. Engaged employees are more productive and committed, and high EI in both leaders and team members can foster an environment where everyone feels valued and motivated. Thus, emotional intelligence is vital in creating a positive and productive workplace, driving overall organizational success.

Guidance for Leaders to Foster Team EI

Lead by Example: Demonstrate high EI in your interactions, showing self-awareness, empathy, and effective communication. Your behavior sets the tone for the team.

Encourage Open Communication: Create a safe environment where team members feel comfortable sharing their thoughts and feelings. Regularly check in with your team and encourage open dialogue.

Provide Training and Resources: Offer workshops and training sessions on emotional intelligence. Provide resources such as books, articles, and online courses to help team members develop their EI skills.

Recognize and Validate Emotions: Acknowledge team members' emotions, whether positive or negative. Show understanding and support, helping them navigate their feelings.

Promote Team-Building Activities: Organize activities that foster trust and collaboration among team members. These can include team-building exercises, social events, and collaborative projects.

Give Constructive Feedback: Provide feedback in a supportive and empathetic way. Focus on behaviors and outcomes rather than personal attributes and offer suggestions for improvement.

Encourage Reflection: Encourage team members to reflect on their emotional experiences and learn from them. Regular reflection can help them become more self-aware and emotionally intelligent.

Support Work-Life Balance: Recognize the importance of work-life balance and encourage team members to take care of their mental and emotional well-being. Support flexible working arrangements where possible.

Celebrate Successes and Learn from Failures: Celebrate team achievements and acknowledge individual contributions. Use failures as learning opportunities, discussing what went wrong and how to improve in the future.

In today's dynamic and diverse work environments, emotional intelligence is vital for leaders and teams. By understanding and managing emotions effectively, leaders and team members can enhance communication, resolve conflicts, build strong relationships, make better decisions, and increase resilience. Developing EI is an ongoing process that requires self-awareness, empathy, self-regulation, social skills, and intrinsic motivation. By prioritizing these areas, leaders and teams can create a more positive and productive workplace, ultimately driving organizational success.

***

Build a Positive Culture

In the modern workplace, leaders play a crucial role that goes beyond driving performance metrics and hitting financial targets. It's about fostering a positive and inclusive culture that values diversity and encourages every team member to bring their unique strengths to the table.

Creating an inclusive culture starts with recognizing and appreciating people's diverse backgrounds, perspectives, and experiences. Diversity isn't just a box to check; it's a powerful asset that drives innovation, enhances problem-solving, and leads to better decision-making. Embracing diversity taps into diverse ideas and insights that might otherwise go unexplored.

Encouraging everyone to contribute their unique strengths is essential in creating an inclusive workplace. When team members feel valued for their individual contributions, they're more engaged, motivated, and committed to organizational goals. This sense of belonging fosters a positive work environment where people are inspired to bring their best selves to work every day.

Leaders play a pivotal role in shaping and sustaining this culture. By modeling inclusive behaviors, providing opportunities for professional growth, and actively addressing any barriers to inclusion, a workplace where everyone feels respected and empowered can be created. This involves being mindful of communication styles, ensuring equitable access to resources and opportunities, and actively seeking diverse perspectives.

Something To Try: Set Cultural Standards

The opportunity is to foster a culture of trust and decisiveness. Several strategies can help navigate this complex landscape:

- **Open Communication:** Strive for transparency in decision-making. Sharing the rationale behind decisions, even when challenging or time-consuming, can demystify the process for team members, mitigating uncertainty and building trust.

- **Set Decision Boundaries:** Establish clear boundaries within which team members can make decisions without escalating them, fostering a sense of autonomy and confidence. It encourages exercising judgment and taking initiative, knowing they have their leader's trust within these defined limits.

- **Encourage Feedback:** Create channels for feedback to allow team members to voice concerns and suggestions about the decision-making process. This can provide valuable insights into the team's perspective, allowing adjustments that enhance clarity and reduce indecision.

- **Cultivate a Fail-Forward Culture:** Champion a culture that views mistakes as opportunities for learning rather than failures to be avoided at all costs. This perspective encourages taking calculated risks and innovating, knowing that the focus is on growth and improvement rather than perfection.

- **Delegate with Trust:** Effective delegation involves more than just assigning tasks; it means entrusting team members with responsibilities and expressing confidence in their abilities to execute them. Leaders should consciously delegate decisively, providing clear expectations and the necessary resources, then stepping back to allow team members to own their projects.

- **Model Decisiveness:** Influence the team's approach to decision-making by modeling decisiveness. This doesn't mean rushing into choices without due consideration but rather demonstrating a balanced approach: gathering necessary information, consulting as needed, making a timely decision, and moving forward.

- **Celebrate Initiative:** Recognize and celebrate instances where team members take initiative and make decisions, reinforcing the value placed on these behaviors. It clearly conveys that taking action is appreciated and supported, even if it involves risk.

- **Recognize and Reward Contributions:** Acknowledge and appreciate team members' efforts and achievements to boost morale and motivation.

As this chapter on empowering teams concludes, it's crucial to acknowledge the profound impact that empowered teams have on overall organizational success and the effectiveness and well-being of leaders. When authority and responsibility are delegated, a culture of trust and ownership is created, allowing team members to thrive and take initiative. This not only enhances performance but also reduces the likelihood of overthinking.

Empowered teams with clear vision and goals, open communication channels, and continuous learning opportunities can operate autonomously. This autonomy supports leaders by distributing the decision-making load, reducing the need for constant oversight, and enabling focus on strategic priorities. Consequently, overthinking significantly reduces, as teams are trusted to handle challenges and make informed decisions.

Furthermore, a motivated and engaged workforce is cultivated by recognizing and rewarding contributions, fostering a positive and inclusive culture, and providing constructive feedback. This engagement leads to increased innovation and problem-solving capabilities within the team, further minimizing stress and over-thinking.

Leading by example and building trust within teams creates an environment where everyone is aligned with the organization's mission and values. This alignment ensures that team members are empowered to act in the organization's best interests. This reduces the need to intervene frequently and allows for a more balanced and focused leadership approach.

12

Bonus: Rules on Failure

Success is not final, failure is not fatal: it is the courage to continue that counts." – Winston Churchill

Failure is a word that often sends shivers down our spines, conjuring up images of catastrophic mishaps and red-faced embarrassment. But let's face it: failure is as inevitable as taxes and the mysterious disappearance of socks in the laundry. My 10 rules on failure are here to help you navigate these unexpected outcomes with humor and grace because, let's be honest, nobody gets through life unscathed.

Embracing failure is empowering and liberating. After all, every mistake is just a plot twist in the epic movie of your life. With these ten rules, you'll discover that unexpected outcomes are not the end of the world but the beginning of a new chapter. They're like those surprise detours on a road trip that leads to unexpected and often hilarious adventures.

The most important rule is the last one. I inherited Rule #10 from my mother, a woman who had no time for self-pity. When life threw her a curveball, she'd throw out a colorful word, take a deep breath, and then declare, "Moving on!" like she was announcing the next stop on a bus route. Her knack for brushing off the unexpected was impressive. Thanks to her, I've learned to handle life's hiccups with a bit of humor and a lot of determination, always ready to move on to the next adventure.

So, let's check out these rules with a smile and a sense of humor. Remember, even the most successful people have their share of facepalm moments. It's how you handle these moments that truly matter. Ready? Let's go! And remember, if all else fails, channel my mom and move on!

Bonnie's 10 Rules on Failure

Rule 1: There are no failures, only expected and unexpected outcomes.

This rule emphasizes a shift in perspective from seeing results as failures to viewing them as outcomes. Each outcome, whether anticipated or not, provides valuable information that can be used to adjust and improve future actions.

Rule 2: No one sets out to fail.

This rule acknowledges failure is never the goal and highlights the intentions behind actions. People aim for success; when things don't go as planned, it's important to remember the original positive intent. This understanding fosters compassion and patience, both toward oneself and others.

Rule 3: Unexpected outcomes highlight flawed understanding.

When outcomes don't align with expectations, it indicates gaps in knowledge or understanding. This rule encourages curiosity and deeper investigation into why things turned out differently, leading to greater insight and refinement of skills or strategies.

Rule 4: There is no shame in not knowing what you don't know.

This rule promotes a healthy attitude towards ignorance, encouraging a mindset open to learning. Admitting gaps in knowledge is not a weakness; it's an essential step towards growth and improvement. Embracing this idea removes the stigma of not knowing and fosters a culture of continuous learning.

Rule 5: Experiential learning is the best learning.

Learning by doing is the most effective way to gain and retain knowledge. This rule underscores the value of hands-on experience in understanding and mastering new skills. It suggests that practical application often teaches lessons that theoretical study cannot.

Rule 6: Unexpected outcomes are designed to be inconvenient.

This rule acknowledges that surprises and deviations from plans often bring discomfort. However, it suggests this inconvenience is purposeful, catalyzing change, adaptation, and innovation. Embracing this discomfort can lead to significant personal and professional growth.

Rule 7: Don't take yourself (or anyone else) too seriously.

Maintaining a sense of humor and humility helps to keep things in perspective. This rule encourages a lighter approach to challenges and setbacks, fostering resilience and preventing undue stress. It reminds us to stay grounded and balanced, even in the face of difficulties.

Rule 8: Unexpected outcomes are nothing to fear.

Fear of the unknown can be paralyzing, but this rule encourages embracing uncertainty. Viewing unexpected outcomes as opportunities rather than threats promotes a more adventurous and courageous approach to life and its challenges.

Rule 9: Unexpected outcomes celebrate beautiful imperfection.

Imperfection is a natural and valuable part of the human experience. This rule highlights the beauty in flaws and the richness they bring to our lives. The Japanese have named beautiful imperfection "wabi-sabi." It encourages accepting and appreciating the imperfect as a source of creativity and uniqueness.

Rule 10: "Moving on!" (aka, Don't Stay Stuck)

Dwelling on past mistakes or setbacks can hinder progress. This rule advocates for resilience and forward momentum. It's a call to learn from the past but not to be anchored by it, promoting a proactive and positive approach to future endeavors.

Conclusion

"What lies behind us and what lies before us are tiny matters compared to what lies within us." – Ralph Waldo Emerson

As we conclude this journey—from grappling with overthinking in leadership to achieving decisive action and clarity—it's important to take a moment to reflect. You've explored the depths of your mind, identifying and understanding the overthinking patterns that once dominated your thoughts. Together, we have moved from recognizing these patterns to implementing tailored, practical strategies that empower you to overcome them.

Central to this transformation is a strong foundation of self-awareness. It helps us identify the triggers that send our thoughts into turmoil. Without this deep self-examination, meaningful change remains elusive in our quest for personal growth.

Throughout our adventure, we introduced strategies—each an element of leadership excellence. From establishing a clear decision-making framework to embracing the calming presence of mindfulness and the robustness of resilience, we've armored ourselves with the tools necessary to combat the specter of overthinking. The significance of physical wellness and the embrace of cognitive behavioral techniques form a holistic shield against the arrows of doubt and indecision.

Let us not forget that emotional intelligence and resilience are the twin pillars upon which impactful leadership rests. These are not mere adornments but the essence of navigating the leadership maze with grace, empathy, and a vision that pierces through the fog of uncertainty.

I urge you to see this book not as a final destination but as a compass—a guide to be consulted as you continue to chart your course through the ever-evolving landscape of leadership. The battle against overthinking is not a skirmish to be won in a day but a campaign—a lifelong commitment to growth, learning, and self-reflection.

I encourage you to share the insights and victories you've garnered from this book with others. Form discussion groups, seek accountability partners, and foster a community of leaders united in their quest for clarity and decisiveness. Sharing our journeys can strengthen us and give us a shared sense of purpose.

In closing, I sincerely thank you for embarking on this journey with me. Your commitment to self-improvement and trust in this book as your guide are gifts of immeasurable value. As you continue to apply the principles and strategies we've explored together, remember that the promise of transformation is real and within reach. The path to becoming a more decisive, impactful, and confident leader is paved with the lessons of our shared journey.

With deepest gratitude and best wishes for your continued growth and success,

Bonnie A. Ross

Spread the Wisdom

"The best way to find yourself is to lose yourself in the service of others." - Mahatma Gandhi

C ongratulations! You now have the tools to be a decisive leader, empower your teams, and drive strategic alignment. But why stop here? Share your newfound knowledge and help other readers discover the same insights.

By leaving your honest opinion of this book on Amazon, you'll guide other leaders to the information they need and inspire them to overcome overthinking.

https://www.amazon.com/dp/196389507X

Thank you for your help. The mission to Stop Overthinking grows stronger when we share our wisdom – and you're a crucial part of this success.

With gratitude- Bonnie

Also By Bonnie

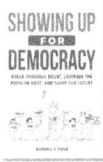

Showing Up For Democracy
Break Through Doubt, Leverage the Popular
Vote, and Shape Our Future

Journal Prompt Poetry
Unlock Creative Flow, Emotional Release,
and Daily Inspiration with the Power of Verse

Stop Overthinking
A Step-by-Step Guide to Letting Go of Mental
Spin to Achieve Inner Peace, Improved
Relationships, and Resilience

Stop Overthinking for Leaders
A Leading-Edge Guide to Decisive
Leadership, Empowering Teams and Driving
Strategic Alignment

Leaving Corporate America
My Top 10 Surprising Discoveries Shifting from
Executive to Entrepreneur

References

- *9 Effective Stress Management Techniques for Leaders* https://www.elevatecorporatetraining.com.au/2019/12/1 8/9-effective-stress-management-techniques-for-leaders /

- Agile Alliance. (2001). "Manifesto for Agile Software Development." Retrieved from agilemanifesto.org.

- Amabile, T. M., & Kramer, S. J. (2011). The Progress Principle: Using small wins to ignite joy, engagement, and creativity at work. *Harvard Business Review Press*.

- American Psychiatric Association. (2013). **Diagnostic and Statistical Manual of Mental Disorders (5th ed.)**. Arlington, VA: American Psychiatric Publishing.

- Appelo, J. (2011). "Management 3.0: Leading Agile Developers, Developing Agile Leaders." Addison-Wesley Professional.

- *Articles, Research, & Case Studies on Decision Making* https://hbswk.hbs.edu/Pages/browse.aspx?HBSTopic =Decision%20Making

- *Avoiding Flawed Decisions: How Leaders Can Overcome Cognitive Biases* https://www.forbes.com/sites/paolacecchi-dimeglio/2023 /07/29/avoiding-flawed-decisions-how-leaders-can-over come-cognitive-biases/

- Beck, K., Beedle, M., van Bennekum, A., et al. (2001). "The Agile Manifesto." Retrieved from agilemanifesto.org.

- Bradberry, Travis, and Jean Greaves. *Emotional Intelligence 2.0.* TalentSmart, 2009.

- Breuer C. Hüffmeier J. & Hertel G. (2016). Does team size matter? A meta-analysis of the effects of team size on performance. Journal of Applied Psychology 101(8) 1414-1438.

- Centers for Disease Control and Prevention. (n.d.). **ADHD Data and Statistics**. Retrieved from https://www.cdc.gov/ncbddd/adhd/data.html

- Cherniss, Cary. "Emotional Intelligence: What It Is and Why It Matters." Annual Meeting of the Society for Industrial and Organizational Psychology, New Orleans, LA, 2000.

- Child Mind Institute. (n.d.). **Obsessive-Compulsive Disorder**. Retrieved from https://childmind.org/guide/obsessive-compulsive-disorder/

- Child Mind Institute. (n.d.). **What is ADHD? Basic Information**. Retrieved from https://childmind.org/guide/what-is-adhd-basic-information/

- Cohen, S., & Wills, T. A. (1985). Stress, social support, and the buffering hypothesis.

- Collins, J. C., & Porras, J. I. (1996). *Built to Last: Successful Habits of Visionary Companies*. Harper Business.

- Conger, J. A., & Kanungo, R. N. (1988). The empowerment process: Integrating theory and practice. *Academy of Management Review*, 13(3), 471-482.

- Covey, S. R. (1989). *The 7 Habits of Highly Effective People: Powerful Lessons in Personal Change*. Free Press.

- Deci, E. L., & Ryan, R. M. (2000). Self-Determination Theory and the facilitation of intrinsic motivation, social development, and well-being. *American Psychologist*, 55(1), 68-78.

- *Decision Fatigue: A Conceptual Analysis - PMC - NCBI* https://www.ncbi.nlm.nih.gov/pmc/articles/PMC6119549/

- Denning, S. (2016). "How to Make the Whole Organization Agile." MIT Sloan Management Review, 58(1), 33-39.

- Doerr, J. (2018). *Measure What Matters: How Google, Bono, and the Gates Foundation Rock the World with OKRs*. Portfolio.

- Dweck, C. S. (2006). "Mindset: The New Psychology of Success." Random House.

- Edmondson, A. C. (1999). Psychological safety and learning behavior in work teams. *Administrative Science Quarterly*, 44(2), 350-383.

- Edmondson, A. C. (2011). Strategies for Learning from Failure. Harvard Business Review. Retrieved from https://hbr.org/2011/04/strategies-for-learning-from-failure

- *Emotional Intelligence and Leadership Effectiveness | CCL* https://www.ccl.org/articles/leading-effectively-articles/emotional-intelligence-and-leadership-effectiveness/

- Gallup. (2013). State of the American Workplace: Employee Engagement Insights for U.S. Business Leaders. Retrieved from https://www.gallup.com/services/176708/state-american-workplace.asp

- Gallup. (2019). Managers Who Delegate Effectively Have Engaged Employees.

- Goleman, D. (2000). Leadership That Gets Results. Harvard Business Review, 78(2), 78-90.

- Goleman, Daniel. *Emotional Intelligence: Why It Can Matter More Than IQ.* Bantam Books, 1995.

- Goleman, Daniel. *Working with Emotional Intelligence.* Bantam Books, 1998.

- Harandi, T. F., Taghinasab, M. M., & Nayeri, T. D. (2017). The correlation of social support with mental health: A meta-analysis. *Electronic Physician, 9*(9), 5212-5222. doi:10.19082/5212

- Harvard Business Review. (2018). The Art of Delegation: How Effective Leaders Empower Their Teams.

- Highsmith, J. (2010). "Agile Project Management: Creating Innovative Products." Addison-Wesley Professional.

- *How Leaders Blend Data And Intuition To Make Better Decisions* https://www.forbes.com/sites/tableau/2023/01/23/how-leaders-blend-data-and-intuition-to-make-better-decisions/

- *How Leaders Can Cultivate a Growth Mindset.* https://www.linkedin.com/pulse/developing-growth-mindset-how-leaders-can-cultivate-overcome-salvi

- *How Leaders Create and Use Networks* https://hbr.org/2007/01/how-leaders-create-and-use-networks

- *How to Move Past "Analysis Paralysis" – 5 Steps for Leaders* https://strategicdecisionsolutions.com/steps-for-leaders-analysis-paralysis/

- Ilies R. Aw S. S. Y. & Pluut H. (2015). Intraindividual models of employee well-being: What have we learned and where do we go from here? European Journal of Work and Organizational Psychology 24(6) 827-838.

- Kniberg, H., & Skarin, M. (2010). "Kanban and Scrum: Making the Most of Both." C4Media.

- Kotter, J. P. (1996). *Leading Change.* Harvard Business Review Press.

- Kouzes, J. M., & Posner, B. Z. (2017). The Leadership Challenge: How to Make Extraordinary Things Happen in Organizations (6th ed.). Wiley.

- *Leader delegation in global software teams* https://www.electronicmarkets.org/fileadmin/user_uploa d/doc/Issues/Volume_22/Issue_01/V22I1_Leader_delegati on_in_global_software_teams_occurrence_and_effects.pdf

- *Leadership Styles: The 11 Most Common & How to Find Yours* https://blog.hubspot.com/marketing/leadership-styles

- Liker, J. K., & Meier, D. (2006). "The Toyota Way Fieldbook." McGraw-Hill.

- Maslach C. Schaufeli W. B. & Leiter M. P. (2001). Job burnout. Annual Review of Psychology 52(1) 397-422.

- Mayo Clinic. (n.d.). **Attention-Deficit/Hyperactivity Disorder (ADHD)**. Retrieved from https://www.mayoclinic.org/dise ases-conditions/adhd/symptoms-causes/syc-20350889

- Mayo Clinic. (n.d.). **Obsessive-Compulsive Disorder (OCD)**. Retrieved from https://www.mayoclinic.org/diseases-con ditions/ocd/symptoms-causes/syc-20354432

- McEwen B. S. (2012). The ever-changing brain: Cellular and molecular mechanisms for the effects of stressful experiences. Developmental Neurobiology 72(6) 565-590.

- *Mindful Leadership Practices For Busy, Distracted Leaders* https://www.forbes.com/sites/amberjohnson-jimludema/ 2021/01/10/mindful-leadership-practices-for-busy-distra cted-leaders/

- National Institute of Mental Health. (n.d.). **Attention-Deficit/Hyperactivity Disorder (ADHD)**. Retrieved from https://www.nimh.nih.gov/health/topics/attention-deficit-hyperactivity-disorder-adhd

- National Institute of Mental Health. (n.d.). **Obsessive-Compulsive Disorder (OCD)**. Retrieved from https://www.nimh.nih.gov/health/topics/obsessive-compulsive-disorder-ocd

- OpenAI. (2024). ChatGPT (May 2024 version) [Large language model]. Retrieved from https://www.openai.com/

- *Overcoming Emotional Overthinking and Over-Analysis in* ... https://www.linkedin.com/pulse/overcoming-emotional-overthinking-over-analysis-deep-dive-patel-obe

- Ozbay, F., Johnson, D. C., Dimoulas, E., Morgan, C. A., Charney, D., & Southwick, S. (2007). Social support and resilience to stress: From neurobiology to clinical practice. *Psychiatry, 4*(5), 35-40.

- *Psychological Bulletin, 98* (2), 310-357. doi:10.1037/0033-2909.98.2.310

- Rigby, D. K., Sutherland, J., & Takeuchi, H. (2016). "Embracing Agile." Harvard Business Review, 94(5), 40-50.

- Rogers, C. R. (1951). Client-Centered Therapy: Its Current Practice, Implications, and Theory. Houghton Mifflin.

- Salovey, Peter, and John D. Mayer. "Emotional Intelligence." *Imagination, Cognition, and Personality*, vol. 9, no. 3, 1990, pp. 185-211.

- Schein, E. H. (2010). Organizational Culture and Leadership (4th ed.). Jossey-Bass.

- Schwaber, K., & Sutherland, J. (2017). "The Scrum Guide." Retrieved from scrumguides.org.

- Scott, K. (2017). *Radical Candor: Be a Kick-Ass Boss Without Losing Your Humanity*. St. Martin's Press.

- Sinek, S. (2009). *Start with Why: How Great Leaders Inspire Everyone to Take Action*. Portfolio.

- Spreitzer, G. M. (1995). Psychological empowerment in the workplace: Dimensions, measurement, and validation. *Academy of Management Journal*, 38(5), 1442-1465.

- Sutherland, J. (2014). "Scrum: The Art of Doing Twice the Work in Half the Time." Crown Business.

- Thomas, K. W., & Velthouse, B. A. (1990). Cognitive elements of empowerment: An "interpretive" model of intrinsic task motivation. *Academy of Management Review*, 15(4), 666-681.

- Tubre T. C. & Collins J. M. (2000). Jackson and Schuler (1985) revisited: A meta-analysis of the relationships between role ambiguity role conflict and job performance. Journal of Management 26(1) 155-169.

- VersionOne Inc. (2019). "13th Annual State of Agile Report." Retrieved from stateofagile.com.

- *Why Top-Leaders Are Practicing Mindfulness - And Four ...* https://www.forbes.com/sites/rasmushougaard/2019/07/08/why-top-leaders-are-practicing-mindfulness-and-four-steps-to-get-started/

- *Why Top-Leaders Are Practicing Mindfulness - And Four Steps to   Get   Started* https://www.forbes.com/sites/rasmushougaard/2019/07/08/why-top-leaders-are-practicing-mindfulness-and-four-steps-to-get-started/

- Woolley, A. W., Chabris, C. F., Pentland, A., Hashmi, N., & Malone, T. W. (2010). Evidence for a collective intelligence factor in the performance of human groups. *Science, 330*(6004), 686-688. doi:10.1126/science.1193147

Disclaimer

Please note that all individual names have been changed to protect the privacy of those involved in sharing insights, themes, and detailed experiences within this content. The participants have been granted permission to share these aspects of their stories, ensuring that personal identities remain confidential. Our commitment to privacy and respect for personal stories is paramount, and we have taken careful measures to preserve the anonymity of all individuals while providing valuable insights and reflections.

www.ingramcontent.com/pod-product-compliance
Lightning Source LLC
Chambersburg PA
CBHW061157120626
46546CB00005B/2101